FEAR NOT!

Meditation and Prayer for the Persistent Seeker

William Clay Manley

ISBN 978-1-0980-2743-8 (paperback)
ISBN 978-1-0980-2744-5 (digital)

Christian Faith Publishing, Inc.
832 Park Avenue
Meadville, PA 16335
www.christianfaithpublishing.com

Printed in the United States of America

Clay, it is an honor to bless your book. I have a master of divinity from Southwestern Baptist Theological Seminary in 1979. And I have a doctor of ministry degree from New Orleans Baptist Theological Seminary in 1989.

Like the ancient Hebrew Psalmists, Clay Manley enlists lofty words that beseech the heavens, lowly words that ordain the routines of the day, and weary words that confess the dark nights of the soul. His words come from a pastor's heart, but they also hold the church's heartbeat in prayer. With human and holy laments, with bold and full praise, and with anguished intercession, these are the congregation's prayers. So let the church say, "Amen."

—Rev. James E Lamkin, D. Min.
Pastor of Northside Drive Baptist
Church, Atlanta, Georgia.

In Clay Manley's *Fear Not! Meditations and Prayers for the Persistent Seeker*, a most important aspect of congregational life is infused with insight and vitality—that of the prayers offered from the worshipping church to God. This is a wonderful resource for those who find themselves chosen for this holy task, but it is equally wonderful as an enhancement to personal devotions. Each is thoughtfully and beautifully written and obviously come from a heart in close and regular touch with God's own heart. I am honored and blessed to have them with me on my journey through life.

—Dr. W. Irwin Ray Jr.
Emeritus Professor of Music
Oglethorpe University

Some people have a "pastoral" voice. These women and men speak in measured tones that manage to convey both warmth and authority at the same time. Anyone who has met Clay Manley knows he is gifted with such a voice. But the prayers collected in this volume are evidence that Clay has the gift of an even deeper pastoral "voice." His openness to the needs of those around him is matched only by his ability to communicate those needs in conversation with God. His words are formal without being stilted; his thoughts are organized without being lifeless. These are the words of a man who is aware that he has no choice but to speak, even though he must speak with "unclean lips."

—Steven M. Sheeley, PhD
BSEd (Political Science/English) from
Missouri State University (1979)
MDiv from Southwestern Baptist
Theological Seminary (1983)
PhD (New Testament) from the Southern
Baptist Theological Seminary (1987)

Author of *Narrative Asides in Luke—Acts* [Bloomsbury, 2015 (Sheffield, 1992)]
Co-Author with Robert N. Nash, Jr. of *Choosing a Bible: A Guide to Modern English Translations (with Robert N. Nash, Jr.)* and *The Bible in English Translation: An Essential Guide (with Robert N. Nash, Jr.).*

Dedicated to my wife, Theresai Mann Manley,
and to our close-knit family:
Children and grandchildren and aunts
and uncles and cousins…
It is a matrix of shared warm strength,
which is a blessing for us all.

Thank God,
Clay Manley

Fear Not!

Every heavenly messenger in the New Testament heralds his message with the same reassuring word— fear not! It is that good news we claim for ourselves this day.

Light of the world and our Good Shepherd, take the fear away:

Fear for family and relatives sick unto dying,

Fear of our own mortality and death close by,

Fear of loss of job, fear of new responsibility,

Fear of loneliness, fear of change, fear of old age.

Take it away Lord, that we might once again lead fearless lives for thee and thy kingdom. Take fear away!

That in thy fearless freedom,

Let the joy of the newborn cry,

Let the joy of personal success duly earned,

Let the joy of friends and family love,

Let the excitement of living our faith.

Ring through us like a bell on a New Year's Day.

Now send us thy message, Lord, to this congregation.

Let each one of us be sensitive to the Lord and obedient to the gospel's will. In the fullness of time, give us the grace to speak boldly. Give us grace enough to hear bravely.

Let the Word be for us, be our manner and our fountain. Brothers and sisters, now is the time to spread the gospel for all to hear. And let the message begin with "Fear not!"

Preface

These prayers are collected from a lifetime of experiences while serving as the pastor of several Protestant congregations.

My responsibilities as pastor included being the worship leader and giving the pastoral prayer. It is from services at these churches that this collection is taken. You will notice that several pieces have been added which are not taken from the primary collection. Included are poems, special services (such as weddings and funerals), and prayers used in small churches attended only once. Let each piece contain its own blessing.

In the introduction to this collection, I suggest several things about prayers about which caution should rule. A casual reading will show that I have not always followed my own ideas. I trust that your patience and understanding will mitigate my shortcomings.

For these sins and more, please forgive me. God already has.

Introduction

Notes and Ideas About Prayer

Prayers come in all sizes, all shapes, and, some, from interesting places. Each religion has its own way to communicate with the Divine. Christian prayers provide us with examples of that variety. They include "high church" prayers, extemporaneous prayers, evangelical prayers. Each one fills a need. This collection of prayers is centered on prayers which are a part of congregational worship services, often led by ordained ministers, as well as by lay leaders.

It has been my experience that these worship leaders are often sincere but ill-prepared for the responsibility of leading congregational prayers. Preparation for this awesome responsibility should include a quiet place for meditation, openness to the many needs of the congregation, and an awareness of the need for Divine guidance in both leader and congregation.

I would not presume to list dos and don'ts in prayer. There are no rules for good or bad prayers. I would, however, encourage all of us to consider these guidelines in public prayer.

Such guidelines could include:

1. What is the Worship Leader trying to do?
   a) Speak for the group.
   b) Gather the thoughts and needs of the group and try to move their focus toward the presence and power of God.
   c) Some prayers form the framework for the various parts of the service, and such prayers are designed to fit that need: Call to Worship, Offering, Benediction, etc. are examples.
2. What is the Worship Leader trying not to do?
   a) Tell the congregation something it does not know as a continuation of the announcements (e.g., "God bless Mrs. Smith in Gwinnett Medical Center in room 313, where she can't have visitors").
   b) Tell God something God doesn't know, in case God has been on vacation (e.g., "Lord, we have been in a drought and need rain very badly").

Suggestions to consider:

1. In your prayers, reflect an acknowledgement of Gender issues. The whole church has much to say and do in confronting these complex issues.
2. Don't use the singular first-person pronoun unless absolutely necessary. "I" is normal for private devotion, but "we" is talking about the whole congregation.
3. Don't "invoke God's presence"! He/She is already there.
4. Don't try to remind or pressure God. God does not forget or neglect or ignore our needs.
5. Asking or begging is okay, not because we can change God's mind but because we need to express our deepest places to the Divine Presence. There is a power in focused spiritual strength.

Always Remember

Praying in public is so difficult that Jesus said we ought not to do it at all (Matthew 6:6). If our public gatherings force us to attempt it, when you finish and go back to your seat, ask God to make you aware of divine patience and forgiveness!

Oakhurst Baptist Church
1988–1994

Invocation

"Breathe on me, breathe on me.
Holy Spirit, breathe on me.
Take thou my heart,
Cleanse every part.
Holy Spirit, breathe on me."

Come, Lord Jesus, come! Breathe on each of us the transforming powerful love of God. Breathe on us, our church family, and our extended family scattered across our land.

Breathe on us all, for we make our prayer in the Savior's name. Amen.

Pastoral Prayer

Lord of the seasons with its heat and bitter cold,
Lord of our good days and celebrations,
Lord of our tears and pain and darkness,
Be for us always—every day, every hour—

Our hope and our constant companion. Steal us
    away
from the gloom that we might live in thy
Light until that "great gettin' up morning" when
all the shadows are banished and we hear the
roll call as the gates of glory are shouted open.
Until that day comes:
Bless the sick.
Bless the care givers.
Bless the families of the sick.
Bless those who stand beside the beds of the dying.
Bless the non-believers who know not of thy abid-
    ing presence—
who know not that the Christ has come,
And
that salvation is at hand.
Bless us all, for we make our prayer in the name of
    Him who taught us, when we pray, to say:
Our Father, who art in heaven, hallowed be thy
    name.
Thy kingdom come, thy will be done, on earth as it
    is in heaven.
Give us this day our daily bread.
And forgive us our trespasses,
as we forgive those who trespass against us.

And lead us not into temptation but deliver us from
evil,

For thine is the kingdom and the power and the
glory forever. Amen.

Oakhurst Baptist Church
June 9, 1988

Pastoral Prayer

Lord God Almighty, maker of heaven and earth, give ear to our
painful supplication.

Creator and sustainer of all we have and are,
Shower us this day with a double portion
Of your patience.

Be gentle with us, Lord!
Our minds are filled with trivia, just like our lives
And our hearts.

We long for thy presence, we need thy grace. We ignore
humility, and we act like tears are for the weak.

It is so hard to get down to praying on a quiet
Sunday morning.
In an age of lovelessness and ugliness, anger and
spiritual starvation,

and families and peoples and nations lost and dying…
Forgive us when we get upset over dust settling on a freshly washed
car!

In an hour of worship—singing, praying, preaching:
When confrontation with the Most High is devoutly to be sought,
forgive us when our lives are filled with concern for what we shall eat
and what we shall wear.
Remind us of all those things that have been put in their rightful place
by the Risen Christ.

Re-clothe us in our rightful minds.
Re-clothe us in rededicated lives!
Prepare us for lives of service and praise.

And we will glorify thy name forever,
And forever,
And forever…

Amen.

Oakhurst Baptist Church
June 26, 1988

Lord God,

The heat and humidity lay as weights on our shoulders in these summer days. And the dust settles on un-watered lawns, and "parched" describes our land and some of our souls.

And it's hard to be Christians of vision and worldwide concern when our focus is repeatedly drawn to whether or not the air conditioning is working.

Lord God,

Once again lengthen our cords and strengthen our stakes "to see the fields white unto harvest"— to see the starving in East Africa, the oppressed in South Africa, the fearful and hate-filled in the Middle East, the doubtful and confused in the Politburo, wondering what Gorbachev will do next.

Lord God,

The litany of need is only exacerbated by our need for thee. Knowing thee, the only true God, as our personal savior is our only sure hope. Ah, but it is so hard for the world to know it when the message has to come through us. Cleanse us, O Lord, and drive us back to the basics to learn once again the joy of sharing the good news of the difference the reality of the power of the risen Christ can make in all our world. Give us soul strength through prayer strength and prayer strength through meditation and communion, that the vast solitudes of the night may speak to us of thy great glory to strengthen us for justice and sacrifice.

Hear our prayer, for we make it in the name of Christ Jesus, who taught us when we pray to say:

Our Father, who art in heaven. Hallowed be thy name.

Thy kingdom come, thy will be done, on earth as it is in heaven. Give us this day our daily bread. And forgive us our trespasses as we forgive those who trespass against us.

Lead us not into temptation but deliver us from evil,

For thine in the kingdom and the power and the glory forever.

Amen.

Oakhurst Baptist Church
December 11, 1988

Give us that portion of thy grace necessary for us—whatever our circumstance—to claim the Advent angel's song as our constant prayer:

"Glory to God in the highest, and on Earth, peace!"
Glory, glory, glory.
Peace, peace, peace.
Let not sickness of self or family or friend,
Let not anxiety over our world or our nation,
Let not fear of success or failure,
Let not joy over triumph—financial or professional
    or personal,
Let nothing still our voices or dampen our spirits as
    we join the angel choirs this glorious season and
    sing to the top of our voices:
"Glory to God in the highest,
And on Earth, peace!"
Glory up there,
Peace down here.

Lord God, let it be our prayer,
And if it be thy good pleasure,
Let it be our song.
Through Christ our Lord,
Amen.

Oakhurst Baptist Church
Christmas Day, 1988

Lord God,

We are made for communion with thee, yet prone to wander.

Lord, I feel it, given to hiding from the voice calling in the evening quiet.

The wandering, the hiding, the voice calling.

Suddenly the creation pauses, and a baby cries.

And God, grown tired of calling, has come looking for us.

In the form of a normal human baby, God has come here.

Love incarnate, impatient with our fickleness, has come searching in the "projects," under the bridges, in the rooms at Egleston, in the emergency room at Grady, on Sunday morning at Oakhurst, in Sanford stadium on a Saturday afternoon.

O Holy Master and Creator of us all,

Give us the grace to turn and answer the calling, still small voice

To fall prostrate at the tear-washed feet...our fear, our loneliness, our only offering, our chance to join the angel choir, our only reward.

Lord God, let our worship this day be a glimpse through a darkening glass, a foretaste of glory to come.

Is our prayer, through Christ our Lord, Amen.

Oakhurst Baptist Church
Martin Luther King, Jr. Birthday Anniversary
January 15, 1989

Pastoral Prayer

Lord God, in thy house are we gathered on this day, a day of memories, a day of commitment.

Memories of violence and marches and "Bull" Conner's dogs, of stirring sermons and rousing speeches, enough to set one's blood a boil.

Memories of years gone by, of great moments in history!

And here we sit, with joys and heartaches of small moment,
little to be remembered, nothing of historical significance.

Births and deaths and sickness and marriage and fear and joy…personal things…the essence of our life together.

Lord God,
So bless us that we can know your presence in our hearts and lives. Minister to our "little" needs, that we might be strong in ministry to the world.

Hear our prayer, calm our fears, still our anxious hearts, strengthen the weak, humble the proud, bless the dying, guide the living.

Through Jesus Christ our Lord.
Amen.

Oakhurst Baptist Church
February 5, 1989

Pastoral Prayer

Lord God,
You have told us to come into your presence like
little children:
Simple, guileless, honest, open.
And we don't do it because we cannot.
Too many years of fooling ourselves,
Too many years of playing church like children
playing house,
Too many years of trying to fool God.

Lord, you must accept us as we are, we can be no
other.
With our anxieties and fears and worries about
health and job,
uncertainty and children and parents and friends…
With egos fired by pride, and sexuality confused
with power,
And growing up is as frightening as growing old…

With our strange ability to separate what we do
    from who we are,
and character and integrity are as rare as the song
    of the
turtledove…
And we rush to worship, trailing clouds of care…

O Holy Master,
In the stillness of this worship hour
Bless and heal and calm and cleanse.
And we will rejoice as the birds of the morning
And sing thy praise forevermore.

Amen.

Oakhurst Baptist Church
February 12, 1989

Pastoral Prayer

Lord God,
You know us each one
Our hairs are numbered,
And our names are known.
In that same personal way, hear our petitions,
Our confessions, our thanksgiving this day.

Bless the ever-growing number of our people whose personal lives need thy blessing. Health is a worry and emotional strength is a need and family can become a dirty word.

Holy Master of us all,
Give us each and every one the grace to quit trying so hard,
At least for this hour, to relax in the sure knowledge of thy redeeming love.

Lord, we are so tired, and the problems so large, give us the blessing of rest and refreshing in this hour of worship.

Give us peace.
Is our prayer through Christ our Lord.
Amen.

Oakhurst Baptist Church
February 25, 1989

Memorial Service

Invocation

Almighty God,
 whose will is sovereign and whose mercy is boundless, look upon us in our sorrow and enable us to hear your word. Help us hear so that, through patience and the encouragement of the scriptures
 We may hold fast to the assurance of your favor and the hope of eternal life,
 Through Jesus Christ our risen Savior.
 Amen.

Pastoral Prayer

Lord God,
We beseech thee for this community of faith and
 this family gathered—blessing upon blessing.

We have been weakened by loss, made uncertain by unwanted change.

For thou hast taken thy servant, Emily Jackson, unto thyself,

And we will never be the same nor our world as bright.

Holy Master, Redeemer,

Heal us of this sorrow, for our journey is long.

Let her life's love and grace and strength be for us as food for our passage and light for paths dark.

And most gracious God...

Begin—even now—to strengthen us that, in God's name and for Jesus's sake, we may go on our way,

Rejoicing and praising thy name forever.

Amen

Oakhurst Baptist Church
February 26, 1989

Pastoral Prayer

Lord God,
Our fountain-source of strength through peace,
Hear our prayers:
Prayers of intercession for the sick and suffering,
Prayers of intercession for world leaders everywhere,
Prayers of thanksgiving for the beauty of flowers
and sunsets
And running horses and ballerinas on point.
For hugs of strength from caring friends.

Hear our prayers of quiet desperation.
Prayers we are afraid to voice aloud, even if only
   God can hear,
For fear the saying of the words will strengthen our
   worst nightmares.

And beyond the hearing, Gracious Master, grant us
   the assurance that we

have been heard.
If we know that you know, it may be that your ter-
    rible silence will be
bearable.

For patience, then, and peace and freedom from
    our paralyzing fears is our
prayer this day.

Creator of mercy and sustainer of hope—hear and
answer.

Through Christ our risen Lord:
Amen.

Oakhurst Baptist Church
March 12, 1989

Pastoral Prayer

Lord God,

Our lives are filled with the joys and sorrows of
    everyday living:
sickness and death
and birth and a new business
and a promotion and a demotion
and a marriage and a divorce,
and anger and fear
the angst of secrets
the ache of sunsets unshared
the pain of empty arms
the joys of a grandbaby toddling.

O Holy One, help us cope with the days and the
    nights.

And beneath the surface of joy and sorrow…out of
   sight,
that dark pool of dread:
formless,
pointless,
waiting,
real,
ready to attach its debilitating energy drain to any
   of life's realities,
And the sewer at the bottom of our soul runs full,
A never-ebbing sea called Anxiety.

Lord God,
Be present in our concerns and our celebrations and
   minister to us as
Thou wilt. And for Jesus's sake, with healing wings
   and hands of love,
be with us in our secret selves. That the anxiety, the
   fear may be
calmed, as on that lake of old, by thy calm, sure
   voice.
For our prayer is made through Christ our Lord,
Amen

Oakhurst Baptist Church
March 26, 1989

Pastoral Prayer

Lord God,
In thy great mercy, we have come full circle,
and again rejoice on an Easter morning.
All thanks and blessing be to thee, oh most high!
For the blessing of life, and for the blessing of
timely death do we give thee thanks.
For health that makes us vigorous and illness that
slows us down, do we give thee thanks.
For the sunshine and the rain
the warm and the cold
Hear our prayers of thanksgiving, Lord Jesus.

In humility and a spirit of supplication do we now
bring our petitions to thy throne of grace.
Of all those for whom we pray:
Some are sick—from colds to cancer, each need
Thy healing presence.

Some are afraid—afraid of life and its chances,
of death and its certainty, some are afraid.
Some are lonely—not enough love, not enough
warm,
never enough close—a loneliness strong enough
to make one cry.
Some are desperate—hemmed in on all sides, they
shout into their darkness with Sartre,
No exit! No exit!

Lord God, in thy limitless love, be present this day
and heal
and bless and comfort and enrich and inspire.

Through Christ our Lord,
Amen.

Oakhurst Baptist Church
April 16, 1989

Pastoral Prayer

Lord God,
The sick—named and unknown—bless them with
an awareness of thy presence.
The emotionally ill—some in hospitals, some not—
fight the loneliest of battles. Bless them with an
awareness of thy presence.
Oakhurst Baptist Church—making momentous
decisions in the midst of change—bless us with
an awareness of Thy presence.

And for those desperate souls who can no longer
feel your presence—too wounded by life, for whom
death appears as a friend, cut off, isolated—if spiritual
calm is no longer reachable:

Oh, Holy Master,
Open their eyes to the world around them.

Help them to see this wave of green that has washed our land in a thousand tints and tones…the grime of winter washed away in
a burst of color called spring.

Lord God,
If lonely folk cannot see Jesus in us, cannot feel
Jesus through
us, or if we lose our way, help us to be a blessing and
a witness.
Give us grace to see resurrection in the world around
us.
Just don't give up Lord. Keep whispering, keep
shouting, keep
Signaling…'til we all hear thy voice and know the
blessed peace
of an awareness of thy presence.

Through Christ our Lord.
Amen.

Oakhurst Baptist Church
April 30, 1989

Pastoral Prayer

Lord God,
It is a day of concern
and our hearts are burdened for those who are ill,
    those who grieve, some who have lost their way.

Our hearts rejoice in the glad good news of new
life coming, of new leadership present, of the dawning of a new day in the life of our church.

Lord God,
So speak to our hearts that we can weep with those
    who weep and rejoice with those who rejoice.
To the glory of God, to the establishing of your
    kingdom here at Oakhurst.

For the brothers and sisters in Christ,
with whom we share our lives.

Through Christ our Lord,
Amen.

Oakhurst Baptist Church
Pentecost
May 14, 1989

Pastoral Prayer

Lord God,
It would help a lot if we could understand!
Understand the voice of the Spirit and its leading.
Understand the power of the Spirit and not fear it.
Understand the presence of the Spirit and open to it.

But understanding is lost in mystery. The Spirit will not be labeled, will not be boxed, will not be controlled
even by our prayer.

Holy Master,
    Give us the strength to let go of our understanding and the grace to open ourselves to the mystery of the Spirit. That from the holy ground on which

we stand, the holy place in which we are gathered, from this holy meeting shall come light and power and fire enlivening our message to an unholy world. We wait upon Thy Holy Spirit.

Through Christ our Lord.
Amen.

Oakhurst Baptist Church
May 28, 1989

Pastoral Prayer

Lord God,
You have called us into thy presence,
As once thou called the mountains from the sea.
You have called us to be thy people,
As once thou called life from the dry ground.
Called us to be thy children,
Inheritors, joint heirs of thy throne.

Why then, Lord, do we feel like aliens, alone in a strange land?
Why, Lord, do we feel like trespassers, violating sacred ground?
Usurpers, pretenders to the sacred throne.

Why, Lord, are we lonely when you are so near?
Why, Lord, are we so guilt-ridden when we are already forgiven?

Why afraid when even death is already conquered?

O Holy Master of us all,
Like a melon ripe for harvest, break us open! Open to healing, open to joy, open to our dependence upon thee.

With saving grace and redemptive love and spiritual power, make us then anew—twice-born, spirit-filled sons and daughters of the Most High! If it be in thy good pleasure, work this miracle here today.

Through Christ our Lord,
Amen.

Oakhurst Baptist Church
June 11, 1989

Pastoral Prayer

Lord God,
From the mystery of thy presence do we come to this life.
We live out our days before thy face.
We journey toward thy peace in eternity.
Thou art all in all;
Our life, our hope, our strength!
Our joy, our rest, our salvation!
Fountain of all love,
Spring of life
Endless source of grace
We do worship and bless thy holy name!

And yet still it is not enough. Our humanness drives us. We must ask for more. We have nowhere else to turn. For healing of body and mind from sickness which so easily besets us, do we most earnestly pray. For forgiveness of sin, done or said or thought, do we most earnestly pray. And on this day do we pray most earnestly for spiritual sensitivity, that we—as a church and as Christian pilgrims— might be ever alert to the leadership of thy spirit.

Come now, Lord Jesus, and forgive and save and heal and lead through the presence and power of thy son Jesus, our Lord and Christ, and the Holy Spirit, our comfort and guide.

Amen.

Oakhurst Baptist Church
June 25, 1989

Pastoral Prayer

Lord God,
Thou hast called us out of darkness into thy marvelous light.
Called us out of coldness into thy wonderful warmth.
Called us out of silence into singing.
Out of loneliness into solitude.

Called us, but not magically transformed us.
We have responded to thy call but only partially.
And our self-induced spiritual schizophrenia continues to tear us apart.
Our Sunday selves are present and praying.
Our weekday selves are silently waiting,
And our selves of unrepentant darkness curse every vestige of light.

O Holy Master of us all,
Who has called us and by thy spirit, call us still.
By thy grace do not lose patience. Continue to call,
continue thy divine invitation until our all, even our
totality is placed on thy redeeming altar—call us beyond desperation to grateful surrender.

Through Christ our Lord,
Amen!

Oakhurst Baptist Church
July 9, 1989

Pastoral Prayer

Lord God,

In humility and humble supplication do we now gather around thy throne in prayer.

We come just as we are and seek earnestly to lay aside all self-serving pretense.

We come just as we are and seek to lay aside our fragmented cares.

We come just as we are—doubting, believing, needing,

lonely, afraid, confident, trusting, singing, praising, cursing, pouting.

O Lord, some days our humanness is almost overwhelming:

So many sick
So many have died
So many lonely
So many lost

God have mercy
Christ have mercy
God have mercy

Adult Choir

Adult Choir
The choral prayer: *Kyrie Eleison* by Thomas Luis de Victoria

Kyrie Eleison
Christe Eleison
Kyrie Eleison

O Holy Master, let thy mercy so engulf us that we can find the grace to transcend what we feel, to be able to truly seek your will and your way for our lives. Our penchant for desiring a problem-solving God is so deep, so strong. Give us the blessing of self-acceptance, and we might find the strength to move through self and its problems to service and its fulfillment.

Through Christ our Lord.
Amen.

Oakhurst Baptist Church
July 16, 1989

Pastoral Prayer

Lord God,

We are so wont to ignore thy presence or deny it. Let our time of prayer this morning center on acknowledgment—acknowledging thy presence in our lives and in our life together. We live and move and have our being in thee, and only there is fulfillment and promise. Hear our prayer humbly confronting thy reality, humbly seeking a greater portion of grateful awareness.

And now hear us as we focus our concern on particular folk in need of special blessings:

Gloria Brooks, Jean Campbell, Ruth Brown, David Harris's father, the family of Mrs. Ola Ray Daniels, those who suffer the ache of personal loneliness, others living with unforgiven guilt, some burdened by the weight of terrible secrets.

Ah, Lord, in ways beyond our understanding, minister to all us with special needs.

And ere we open our eyes from this prayer, impress upon us all the difference between the sickness some of our congregation suffers and the sickness unto death, with which we all must deal. Forgive our sin, fill our lives with grace, confront each of us with our mortality and our hope in glory. Grant us the assurance of our second birth, here we fail before our first death. And in thy presence and in the light of thy redemption and the confidence of thy salvation, will we worship and praise thy name this day, and throughout all the ages, world without end.

Amen.

Oakhurst Baptist Church

Lord God,

Winter is a distant memory, and the flowers of Spring long gone. Humidity, heat, thunder, lightning, and rain and even the summer is far spent, and we are not saved. Lord God, we are not saved…

Not saved from short-sighted ignorance…

Not saved from power-hungry politicians or paranoid military leaders…

Not saved from those who put money before morality and self before everything.

We befoul our nest as we befoul our souls, and knowing better doesn't mean doing better.

Lord have mercy upon us. Lord have mercy.

(Choir: Kyrie Eleison)

Lord God,

We are not saved from the physical and mental anguish to which our human frailty is heir. Some of us are sick, physically sick:

Gloria Brooks, Tom Hall, Jean Campbell.

Some of us are angry, some broke, some desperate, some out of work, some frustrated with work, and some would give all that they have and are to avoid one more lonely night. Some are worried about family or friends. Some feel guilty about good fortune. And "why me?" is either a prayer or a curse.

In all these souls, with all their manifold needs, in all these bodies, with all their physical ills, in this congregation, with all its needs and frustrations and aspirations and dreams...

Christ, have mercy upon us. Christ, have mercy! (Choir: Christe Eleison)

Lord God,

Summer is ending and winter is past and we are not saved from anxiety and despair. Our best efforts seem to have no effect, and nothing we do seems to help. The sea of life is so large, and our ship is so small. It is a billion miles to the nearest star and a billion people are hungry and a billion people are oppressed and a billion oppressing, a billion sins unacknowledged, unconfessed.

We don't know what to do about any of it, and we grow so weary in well-doing, and it seems so futile...

Lord have mercy upon us Lord have mercy, have mercy, have…

(Choir: Kyrie Eleison)

O Holy Master,

Grant us the blessing of patience and courage and hope. Give us a vision and a dream.

Fill us with the strength of silence and the glory of the power of praise.

We wait for the leadership of thy Spirit.

And our prayer is made in the name of him whom to know is life eternal, even Jesus the Christ, our Lord.

Amen and Amen.

Oakhurst Baptist Church
All Saints Sunday
November 6, 1989

The Prayer of Remembrance

Lord God,
All Saints Sunday has come 'round again,
and, for some of us,
the year past has been a year of tears.
Good times, yes, and laughter
Quiet times, yes, and deep searching.
But good times and quiet can be drowned,
lost to memory in a year of tears.

Too many deaths, and none without pain…
And the loneliness of living becomes a stake
in the heart, pierced through with sharp loss.
And unshared joy lies curdling in our souls
like milk in the sun.
And silence rules the night.

But it's time now to move beyond the pain,
time to lay our sorrow down, Lord,
time to step back and gain perspective,
time to remember the good…rejoice in the blessings,
and come to terms with the loss.
Time to "get ahold of ourselves," say well-meaning
friends.
Ah no! Ah no!

It's time to be grasped by God,
time to lean on the everlasting arms,
time to let the dead sleep in Jesus,
while we walk with Him, arm in arm.

Oh Holy Master,

It is time for your grace:
To receive it, we need your transforming power.
So come now, Lord Jesus,
and make this All Saints Day our day of reawakening.
Give us the power to live with the pain,
life once again abundant and triumphant.

"Abundant and triumphant"?
We can't do it Lord,
we don't know how to live abundantly and alone.

We must have your blessed presence.

So come by here, my Lord, come by here.
Ere we, too, die!
Some of us are praying, Lord, some of us are crying,
Some of us are singing, Lord, some of us are dying.
Kum-bah-yah, Kum-bah-yah, Kum-bah-yah.

In your presence will our salvation be made real,
And joy will come in the morning.

Kyrie Eleison.
Amen.

Oakhurst Baptist Church
July 1, 1990

Pastoral Prayer

Lord God,
In the quiet of the morning,
Do we acknowledge thy presence,
seek thy guidance, plead for thy peace.

Ah, Lord,
the hot, dreary "dog days" of August
have come early this year, and the humidity
is as welcome as a wet wool blanket in July.
And the depressing weather is but a symbol
for the spiritual load many of thy children bear.
Lord, some of us in this room experience
the "dog days of August" year-round, every year.
Illness and misfortune and loneliness and despair
rob some of us of hope and happiness and fulfillment.
The "joy of salvation" is hard to know, gone with
childhood's dreams.

Lord God Almighty.
Use your strength, in the name of your grace and
   compassion,
to "open our eyes that we may see, glimpses of truth
thou hast for us"…and not only truth, but hope, and
community.
God, help us to see the love, expressed and waiting,
alive on every hand.

And Lord God, if it be in thy good pleasure,
open the eyes of those of us for whom joy is a daily
   reality,
to see the many for whom a hug is a handle on
   sanity,
that we might be a channel for your blessing
to a lonely, loveless world.

And beyond these walls, there are sick to be blessed,
joy of new life to be shared, death to be grieved over,
exciting lives for young people to plan and live.
Politics and power, hunger and war, adventure and art,
a universe to explore, and an earth to exploit.

Holy Master,
In the day to day drama of living,
In the night to night hell of loneliness.
Be thou our vision, our guide, our stay.
Thou Christ our Lord,
Amen

Oakhurst Baptist Church
November 4, 1990

Pastoral Prayer
Evensong

Lord God Emanuel,
Lord of Lords, Light of Lights
Keeper of the sunrise beyond the darkness...
Thou fountain of hope, wellspring of joy
Thou who has given us grace abounding and peace
in times long past...hear our prayers this day!

For in the quiet of Evensong, we find a name for
    our
disease...and that name is loneliness.
So many from among us gone...
so many moved away, but here's the rub,
so many dead...so many dead.
Leaders and followers, workers and prayers, givers
    and keepers
And faithful. Lord God A'mighty, who among us

can walk in the footsteps of faithfulness laid down
by the likes of Ada Barker and Emily Jackson and
    Ethel Johnson
Or who can smile like Gloria Brooks, who has the
    bright
promise of Mark Smith?
And the empty seats in this room are daily remind-
    ers of
the damnation that is loneliness.

O Holy Master of us all,
We call upon your boundless grace…
In the name of your Son, our Savior, Jesus of
    Nazareth,
our risen Redeemer and Lord,
Save us from the abomination of desolation,
this loneliness that eviscerates even the strongest.
Save us, Lord! Save us now!

And when the loneliness is finally hemmed in with
    the love,
Speak to us, in ways each of us can understand,
that we might be emboldened to step forward
and fill the ranks for those now gone.
Our time to lead, to serve, to smile, to give…our
    time, our time.

our time, our time

And if we be found faithful servants in our time—
One reward we ask, and that with all our hearts…

When the saints named here today go marching in,
Marching into your presence,
O Lord, let us march too.
Shoulder to shoulder, arm-in-arm
With Emily and Ada and Mark and all the rest
Singing the songs of Zion into the church
    triumphant.

O Lord, we want to be in that number
When these Saints go marching in.

Grant it Lord, Let it be
Through Christ our Lord.
Amen.

Oakhurst Baptist Church
February 3, 1991

Prayer for "Outer" Vision

Lord God,
It is for a clearer vision of the world we pray—
humanity's pain and suffering and hunger,
hopelessness etched deep in lined faces,
children with lackluster eyes and bloated bellies…

Have mercy on us, Good Master, for it is so hard.
Our spiritual myopia is fueled, not with too little,
but with too much.
Seeing so much suffering, we see none at all.
Hearing so much crying, we hear none at all.
New crises day by day, wars and rumors of wars…
and some of us feel guilty for having forgotten
Central America in the maelstrom of the Persian
    Gulf.

Give us a vision, Lord, a vision of your world,

and light it with resurrection morning sun.
Cleanse our souls of our addiction to the TV news,
that our seeing may be defined, not by strobe lights,
but by the sharp outlines of a shadowed cross.

For your prophet was right, Lord. Without vision
    we perish!
Give us eyes to see, ears to hear…
that amidst the cacophony of sound bytes and rap
    music
and morning traffic and the gut-wrenching fear of
    losing
our joy and unpaid bills and growing old and being
unpopular at school and not getting a Valentine…

Ah, Holy Master, give us a double portion of thy
    boundless grace,
that we might once again be empowered to see the
    bush enflamed,
to hear the still, small voice,
to live our lives as if today was that "great getting-up
morning."

Take away our fascination with the tramp of armies
    massed!
Center us, focus us, renew our strength!

We march not to drums beating, but to choirs
    singing…
and the city of God is our goal!
Lord God, enlarge our hearts, define our vision,
that we might invite the whole world to share with us
both the journey and the song.

For we make our prayer in the name of Him whom
    to know
is life eternal…
Even Jesus Christ our Lord.
Amen.

Oakhurst Baptist Church
August 18, 1991

Pastoral Prayer

Lord God,
Into thy presence we come;
seeking strength through quietness,
seeking forgiveness through repentance,
inspiration through music,
comfort in shared compassion,
companionship in a warm hug.
Here we are, and we can't break through to any of
    our needs
because we are still dragging last week behind us…
bosses and bills and burdens and bunions,
and triumphs and parties and promotions.
Holy Master, we couldn't concentrate on you
even if the rapture broke around us.

Lord God, grant us that portion of thy grace
    necessary

to empower us to lay down our burdens at your
   altar.
Let love cut us loose or glory free us…
whatever it takes…
Bless us with a focused hour…
And a lighter step on our journey.

Through Christ our Lord,
Amen!

Oakhurst Baptist Church
October 10, 1993

Pastoral Prayer

Lord God,
these are the best of times
these are the worst of times
and our laughter and our tears are all mixed up.

Peace is coming to Palestine…
Apartheid is leaving South Africa…
Ecological awareness increases daily…
The groans of freedom aborning fill the air.
Thank you God for this new day!

Somalia is being destroyed…
Bosnia is self-destructing…
Armenia and India shudder with pain…
And an awful lot of children in Georgia go to bed
    each night
neglected and hungry and afraid.

God, there is no newness, it's the same old stuff!
Why have you left us to suffer…alone and lost?

Holy Master of us all,
Set us free from the spiritual rollercoaster called
the daily newspaper and the evening news.
Deliver us from presidents and princes and
    parliaments
and marching armies…wars large and small.

In the name of Jesus of Nazareth—Save us!
Open our eyes to sin.
Remind us of forgiveness and
Refresh us with saving grace.

Almighty God
Let the power of the Gospel set us free—
that we might be, once again,
light and salt and leaven,
and beacons a-shining to this lost and hurting world,
that we might once again feel and know
the joy of our salvation.

For we make our prayer in the name of Him for
    whom the confusion

of laughter and tears was as common as daily
   bread…
Even Jesus Christ our Lord.

Amen!

Oakhurst Baptist Church
January 2, 1994

Pastoral Prayer

Lord God
The holiday season draws to a close,
And some of us are already tightening our belts,
gearing up to get back in the rat race.
For some, the emotions of family and festivity are
    still very real.
Emotions to struggle with as much as to enjoy.
With hearts full and minds distracted and emotions
    quite on edge,
Do we come into thy house this day for worship.

Lord God
Grant us all that portion of thy grace necessary…
Necessary for us to breathe in slowly and deeply of
    thy peace.
Grace enough for us to claim thy promise of the
    easy yoke and

the light burden.
Grace enough to understand and forgive and never
    let go of
loved ones dying.
Grace enough to understand and forgive and never
    let go of loved ones living.
Grace enough to ignore the personal slight,
the abrasive rudeness of our interpersonal world.
Grace enough to forgive ourselves,
forgiveness for missing the mark…
forgiveness for missing the mark and not giving a
    tinker's dam
for the missing of it,
forgiveness for just not caring.
Grace enough to once again discover the joy of our
    salvation!

Lord God Almighty
With grace enough and peace,
And loads lightened by forgiveness,
Lead us into this New Year
With spirits strong and
Hearts equal to the task.
Rich in love
Abounding in mercy
Faithful to our calling.

For we make our prayer in the name of Him whom to
    know is to follow:
Our Leader
Our Lord
Even Jesus of Nazareth, the Christ.
Amen

VESPERS

February 4–April 29, 1990

Vespers
February 4, 1990

Pastoral Prayer

Lord God,
This day is far spent, and darkness is upon us.
Night comes quickly and too quickly for pilgrims
    on the road.
Too many things to do, too few hours
The responsibilities get larger, but the hours never do.
The frustrations mount in geometric progression.
Do more, be more, make more, sell more
Be better citizens, be better Christians, be better
    parents, be better children
Give more money, give more time, give more self.

Ah Lord Jesus,
In the cool of this winter's evening
Give us the grace to decompress,
to take the evening shadows,
and wrap ourselves in their quietness.

Grace to relax, and accept sleep when it comes.

"Peace, peace, marvelous peace,
Peace, the gift of God's love."

And in the morning, we will claim the light for our
   own!
In its glory, redeem the day!
As we seek to follow Him who is crowned the Lord
   of Light
and our salvation.
Even Jesus Christ
Amen.

Vespers
February 11, 1990

Pastoral Prayer

Lord God,
You have brought us into this world
and make us a part of it...
Heirs to all its joy and beauty,
its disease and danger, death and despair.

Hear us now as we pray, pray from the
depths of our humanness, where deep calls to
     deep...
Bless and strengthen the sick
Encourage those hurt by the storm,
Comfort the families of the dead,
Be present with the discouraged.

With thankful hearts do we acknowledge
Mandela's freedom, and every expression
of the revival of human spirit around the world.
Praise thy name, O Most High.

O Holy Master, teach us patience,
Patience to accept our humanness, our frailty.
Patience to wait for your presence, your strength,
and peace to enjoy the blessing of our world and
     your
kingdom.

Through Christ our Lord,
Amen.

Vespers
February 18, 1990

Pastoral Prayer

Lord God,
Hear our prayers this night…
For sick people alone,
For searching people afraid,
For good people lost,
For angry people, and sad…
desperate and hungry…
one sleepless night too many…
One put-down, one careless disparaging remark too
    many!
For those learning the meaning of "being hurt,"
For those learning the bitter taste of "getting even,"
For those who missed the promotion,
and for those in a job where there are no promotions.

O Holy Master of us all,
Work miracles where miracles will help!

Say no when we do not know what's good for us!
Shut up our pious chatter with your silence!

"Holy, Holy, Holy, Lord God of Hosts
Heaven and Earth are full of thee,
Heaven and Earth are praising thee,
O Lord most high!"

Give us voice to join in that chorus.

Through Christ our Lord.
Amen.

Vespers
March 18, 1990

Pastoral Prayer

Lord God,
Thou hast made us in thine image,
souls fit to grow as large as the universe.
Great capacity for love,
Great capacity for compassion,
A place to hold grace for a lifetime,
And hope and forgiveness for an eon.

Then why, Lord, why?
Why such smallness,
such littleness, such paucity in our lives?
Our strength lasts but for the morning, and the
noonday heat finds us empty!
And the world beats a path to our door…
show love, share hope, teach forgiveness.
Must we send them empty away?

O Holy Master,
So empower, so enrich us with thy indwelling spirit,
that we can be the people you would have us be,
face the destiny for which we were created.
Lord, make us salt for the whole earth,
and light—
Let grace abound!
Build our reputation on love...
And give us the grace, in the quietness of this worship time,
to open our hurts and needs and anger and fears to
thy
healing touch,
to prepare us for these our appointed tasks.
Grow us as big as the need, and as strong...

Through Christ our Lord,
Amen

Vespers
April 1, 1990

Pastoral Prayer

Lord God,
Our life is too much with us.
Pressures of job…
Anxieties of living…
The family matrix as often
the problem as the solution.
Friends die, or desert us.
New friends come,
But the angst of loneliness,
the spectre of alone and no one to help, haunts our
    quiet places.
And the problems are never solved over and done.
They merge and blend and interweave
and go on forever, often like bad soap opera.
Little peace, little rest, little calm.

O Holy Master,

Give us focus! Center our lives, direct them, and let them be centered on thee:

To the end that out of simplicity and togetherness, focus and direction,

Shall come strength for the journey and hope and the joy of our salvation.

Set us free!

Through Christ our Lord,
Amen.

Easter Vespers
April 15, 1990

Pastoral Prayer

Lord God,
It has been a glorious Easter Day
with flowers and birds
and a thousand tints and tones of new green.
Spring celebrates new life with every breath,
even the stones sing of rebirth.

O Holy Master,
Bring nature's song to our hearts.
Lead us into springtime in our souls.
Take spring's celebration of rebirth,
and show us new birth.
Stir the deep places, revitalize the slow,
Teach us how to sing once more
in thy good pleasure,
And if it is not the right time or place
for celebration and dance…
Then teach us how to pray

Prayer of thanksgiving
Prayer of intercession
Prayer of confession
Prayer of hope
Prayer for peace
Through Jesus Christ our Lord!
Amen.

Vespers
April 29, 1990

Pastoral Prayer

Lord God,
The mystery is why you put up with us,
Century after century, millennia on end,
Stubborn or hard-headed or dumb or sinful,
The limits of thy patience must stretch through
    time
and beyond.

Lord, we want so much to have it our way…
we want to understand the message
and control the messenger
And keep the power in our hands.

It's so hard when we don't comprehend love
and can't do anything to gain your favor.
When all we've got is us.

Holy Master hear our prayers.
If it be in thy good pleasure,
give us the grace to accept the Word you have sent,
to love the Messenger you have sent,
and to worship thy name forever.

Now comfort the distressed.
Minister to the lonely.
Calm the disturbed.
Warm cold hearts.
Bless this hour.

Through Christ our Lord,
Amen.

Loganville Christian Church
2005–2011

Loganville Christian Church
May 7, 2006

Restore the Kingdom?

Invocation

M ost Holy and most loving God,
On this Lord's Day do we lift our voices in praise
and thanksgiving,
in adoration and petition…
Let all the earth be filled with worship.
Let every joyful heart be heard.
Let every need-filled heart be blessed.
Let every lonely heart be warmed.
Attend to us, everyone, and we will praise thy name
forever.
Amen.

Pastoral Prayer

"Come we that love the Lord, and let our joys be
known.
Come we that doubt the Lord, and let our angst be
known.
Come we that ignore the Lord, and let our disdain
be known."

Holy One Most High
Give us grace enough to throw wide the doors of
our church
and welcome all—saints and sinners alike—to this
house of peace and
perspective. Show us how to spread wide the news
of your free and
freeing love. Make us as accepting as Christ Himself.
Teach us how to serve
thee best, that others may know thy forgiveness and
love.

Now hear us as we pray for our sick…
Now hear us as we pray for our leaders…
Now hear us as we pray for our homeless and
jobless…
Now hear us as we pray for those who grieve…

With all these needing hearts, make this thy church a place of comfort and hope. Make us thy people, servants and servers of God's love and God's acceptance and God's peace.

For our prayer is made in the name of Him who taught us, when we pray to say, "Our Father."

A Meditation

Restore the Kingdom

The pain was real and pervasive. Pain joined by heartache, nurtured by defeat. It had been so for many, many years. And gradually the realization emerges that events, left to themselves, are not going to get better. This pain is not going to fade away. Each new generation births its own hell. Every day's evil proves to be sufficient for that day, and the stockpile of the anguish grows. What we need is a leader. God needs to send us a great leader who will bring back the "good old days." Like it was when David was king, only better. What we need is a Messiah! Someday, God will send us one. It was seven hundred years before Christ's birth. The dream was born. Simple and to the point, the dream said, "No matter how bad things get, don't give up; because God is going to send us a Savior—a Savior who will lead God's people back to glory."

Now, not all of God's prophets had the same idea about the coming Savior. Some said that he would be a different kind of king in a different kind of kingdom. Second Isaiah said that he would be a suffering servant, whose pain would be for our healing. First Isaiah said that he would be a wonderful counselor, a mighty God, an everlasting Father, a Prince of Peace. Not a word in the four titles suggests armies or money or power. But these cautionary voices were soon drowned out by the people's clamor for relief from losing wars and slavery and deportation. They needed a dream, so they made one to fill their needs. In the seven hundred years before Christ came, the pain got bigger and the dream got clearer. "God is going to deliver us from all this—deliver us by a great leader, deliver us to power and prestige and money. When the great day comes, Jerusalem is going to be the capitol of the whole world."

The disciples shared the dream with everyone else. Everyone knew it, and everyone believed it. And then Jesus came! Wise teacher, miracle worker, leader…perhaps…perhaps he is the one to come. Maybe not. His teaching and actions didn't fit the mold. "Perhaps he is just getting ready to break out and get things started."

And then the crucifixion—bitter disappointment and defeat.

And then the glorious resurrection.

Hallelujah! Even death has been conquered.

Wounds can be healed, death overcome. Forget what he said. Forget the humble Rabbi washing our feet. This is our chance. Everyone will be willing to join our army. The hated Romans will be easily defeated. And so, at the first opportunity, the sure question, "Lord, is this when you are going to restore the kingdom?"

The gospels mention on one occasion Jesus weeping. I have an idea that Jesus wept more than once, and I would not be surprised if this was one of those times. This is either time for tears or beating your head against the wall. Hadn't the disciples understood anything in his three years of teaching? Jesus had not come to lead victorious armies in proud array into a new Jerusalem! He had not come to build a kingdom in which his followers would be rich! He didn't care about those material things. As a matter of fact, he repeatedly said that material successes and comforts were a tremendous problem, a burden, an impediment to the coming New Days. No! He came to lead us all back to God. He came to revolutionize our lives and save our souls. Who is king and who has money and who has power were side issues of little importance. It doesn't much matter who is king. It does matter whether or not you have spent time today in prayer. Do you love your neighbor? Do you love the Christian fellowship? That is the kind of thing that is important to Christ. And the disciples had missed the whole point of Jesus's life and ministry. Surely, it was yet another time for Jesus to weep.

Boy, these disciples were surely dumb, weren't they? Spiritually thick-headed. Couldn't they see what Jesus was about? No, they couldn't, and it was not because they were dumb. They shared with us the human frailty of holding on to any idea, once planted in our minds, with a death grip, even if later evidence proves it wrong. They inherited an idea seven hundred years in the making. It was an idea that fulfilled their wishes and their hopes and their fantasies. No! They couldn't give up the idea of Messiah as king in any three years of teaching. They didn't give it up after conversation with the risen Christ. It took the Holy Spirit at Pentecost to start turning the disciples around. Don't feel superior! Two thousand years with the Holy Spirit in our midst, and we still do the same things they did.

We, like the disciples, just love to hold on to mistaken ideas, no matter the evidence. Especially ideas that arise out of our culture. We latch on to them and then bring them over to our churches and call them Christian ideas. The most obvious one has to do with "success" and what defines it. Our culture, our society is built upon the goal of winning—winning at whatever game or contest or business in which we might be engaged. As sports coaches are so prone to teach us, winning isn't everything, it is the only thing. We don't play sports games in this society, for the fun of playing and the excitement of competing: we play to win. Everything becomes a game, even if we have to invent a way to keep score. We play to win, and nothing else matters.

Take that idea, which is reinforced by our society at every turn, and bring it over into the church. How do you play the game of church? You use every level where you have numbers. The church wins if it has the most people or the most churches or the most money or is growing the fastest or has the most activities. If you can count it, you can compare it with other churches, and the game is on. Preachers endorse and support the game, especially if they are in one of the big growing congregations. And competition breeds jealousy, breeds disillusionment, breeds discontent. "Maybe we need a new coach" is a logical response to losing the game. And it all starts when cultural values are absorbed into the church, and the church and the culture come ever closer and closer to merging into one entity. When that happens, the culture does not cease to be the culture, but the church ceases to be the church. The New Testament says that we ought to be in the world but not of the world. We have a track record of eliminating all such distinctions. And more and more, the church and the culture become identical—just like the disciples wanted two thousand years ago.

Truth to tell, maybe that would make things simpler. Let's go ahead and merge church and culture. It would get rid of some embarrassing complications for Christians. You see, under normal circumstances, we don't like the Christian life anyway. We don't admire the Christian virtues. And most of all, we don't want to be made to feel guilty just because we don't like them. We don't fill up our churches seeking humility and peace and learning how to forgive others and patience and a chance to wash our enemies' feet. We admire strength and money and power and success. We like a winner.

Christianity talks about losing and weakness and quiet retreat and plenty of prayer and being poor.

This tragedy has happened time and time again. Dissatisfaction with the traditional Christian life leads to the absorption of more popular ideas into the church. The church and the culture become identical, and the job of the church becomes to put the stamp of divine approval on people living the way they want.

In Nazi Germany, in the 1930s and 1940s, there was rampant prejudice against the Jews. The Jews were blamed with everything that had gone wrong. So the Germans decided to use their soldiers to kill all six million Jews. And not a word of protest came from the church. A handful of rebellious pastors raised their small voices, but the official church stand on the issue was silence. And on every German soldier carrying out those awful orders was a belt buckle stamped with the phrase, "God With Us." Church and culture were one.

The Southern Baptist Convention was formed because the American Baptists came out against slavery. Our Southern culture and society was built on slavery. Nobody likes to think their society is built on sin, so you get the church to say that God says that everything is okay, that how you are living and how you want to live is God's will. The church and culture's being one is the foundation stone upon which the Southern Baptist Convention was built.

It has happened over and over again in every culture in every era, and it is happening all over the Atlanta Metro today. Who of our generation is going to speak up and ask the twenty-first century's version of the age-old question, "Lord, is this when you are going to restore the kingdom?" Are we close enough to the merging of our church with our culture, for that to be a realistic question? You know that we are! Hear Reinhold Niebuhr:

"There is a view [very popular in twenty-first century America] that insists on a God without wrath, bringing men and women without sin into a kingdom without judgment through a Christ without a cross."

God save us from ourselves, for as Pogo says, "We have met the enemy and he is us."

God help us! God, save us from ourselves!

Amen!

May 25, 2008
Prayers

Invocation

All holy and all wise God, into thy house do we come this day, seeking blessing and guidance.

We need thy love and thy understanding and thy forgiveness.

We need thy guidance and thy leadership and thy patience when we stray.

It is to thy house that we come, for we have nowhere else to turn.

Let our worship be acceptable to thee and thy response a bounty of blessing.

For we make our prayer in the Savior's name. Amen.

Pastoral Prayer

Creator God,

Hear our prayers this day. We have sick and depressed and discouraged folk in our church family. We have lonely and frightened ones as well. So much spiritual hunger. We need thy presence in power. Come, Lord Jesus, and fill our assembly with thy powerful love.

Bless all those for whom we should pray. Accept our thanks for our heroes who have given the last full measure of devotion. Hear our prayers for the families and friends of those now gone from us. Let this Memorial Day be for all of us a renewal of our loyalties, a renewal of our commitment, and a pledge to work for peace.

Hear our prayers, for they are made in the name of Jesus.

Loganville Christian Church
May 25, 2008

A Meditation
Catch 22

Is anyone here familiar with the novel, *Catch 22*? It was written about 1960. It is a novel about World War II. The hero, if you can call him that, is a pilot flying bombing missions over Germany. He has had enough of war and is trying to get out. He decides to claim mental impairment and wants to apply for a medical discharge on the basis of his being "crazy." He discovers that he must fill out a form applying for the discharge. When he does so, he is turned down. It seems that if you had enough sense to fill out the form, you must not be crazy. The form was number 22.

Now, "catch 22" is a part of our language. It always identifies an absolutely hopeless situation—where the rules are set up to make progress impossible.

Today is the second Sunday after Pentecost. I have been reading in that part of Acts between Pentecost and Paul. A marvelous portion of that Scripture is the sermon Stephen preached before he was stoned to death. In the sermon, Stephen reminds his accusers—the High Priests—of their shared history. Stephen tells of Abraham and Isaac and Jacob and Joseph, of Moses and the "burning bush," of Sinai and the building of the tent to be the Tabernacle of God. The Tabernacle was built according to God's specifications as reported by Moses. This portable house of God was brought through the wilderness for those forty long years. When the Israelites came to Canaan, the Tabernacle tent was again set up. It was the place where God dwelled. David and Solomon came along a couple of hundred years later, and the portable Tabernacle tent was replaced by the permanent abode of God— the Jerusalem Temple. Made of stone and large for its time, it was a fit dwelling place for God.

It is ever and always so. In just about every religion the world over, we, all people, need for our God to have a place. There are thousands of them. The largest, most grand house of God I have ever entered is the Cathedral of St. John the Divine in New York City. It is, I was told, the largest cathedral in the world. It is an amazing place. The smallest active church house I have seen was less than half the size of our church. Size makes no difference. People need a place to gather where they are most likely to contact the presence and power of God. We call it God's house—the place where God lives.

And inevitably over time, every single one of us wants God to stay there. Stay in your house, we will come to see you Sunday. Don't come to the night club. Don't come to the dance. Don't come to the ball game. Don't come to the school.

And everybody knows that that will not work. God is not, not ever going to stay in the house we build for him.

Even the Jews knew that five hundred years before Christ. Stephen quotes Isaiah 66:

> Thus says the Lord;
> Heaven is my throne and the earth is my footstool;
> What is the house which you would build for me,
> And what is the place of my rest?
> All these things my hands have made,
> And so all these things are mine, says the Lord.

You wish to build God a house. The heavens, the stars, and the moon are his throne, and the whole earth is but his footstool. How large a house will it take to contain God? Isaiah knew that the very idea was ridiculous, and Isaiah lived five hundred years before Christ.

We know that too. We know that no physical house can ever contain God, even if it be a cathedral. Churches and cathedrals are built for us and not for God. But humanity will not give up. We will build a house for God. We must. And if not out of wood and stone and glass then out of doctrines and forms of worship and sacred music. All this and more circumscribe God. We can define God with our theologies and mold his environment with our seminary-trained ministers, with our hymns, and with our doxologies. It is humanity's built-in nature. We cannot change. We must organize our world and our thoughts, our religion and our sports. It is our nature.

And it is all for naught. God will not be trapped in a house, and he will not be defined by our theologies. No matter how many libraries we fill with learned tomes, God Almighty moves as the wind and is just as easy to control. It is a perfect Catch 22. We build

God's house because we must—a house of words or a house of wood. We build because God made us that way. And it never works. It is a "catch 22."

Have you heard of the British Bible scholar who was one of the first to publish the New Testament in modern English? His name is J.B. Phillips, and he published it in about 1950. He is known for his translation work, but he also wrote some general religion books, and his best one is *Your God is Too Small*. It is not a large book, but its message is large indeed and deep. It speaks directly to us this morning. In the title of his book, he defines our problem—our God is too small.

We want God to be small enough that we can be comfortably casual in his presence. We want God to be small enough that our image of him can be one of a wealthy, powerful, kindly grandfather, and we are all favored grandchildren.

We want God to be open and totally understandable—never any mystery.

We want God to be instantly available, especially when we have a problem—always at our beck and call.

We have not made God into the image of a golden calf, and Aaron did. We have made God into an idealized father figure. And everything is going to turn out just fine, thank you.

God forgive us. God have mercy on us. Our God is a slightly larger version of ourselves. If we can't be God, we'll make God like us.

Shame! Shame on us all! Where is the God of history? Where is the God of the storm? Where is the God of the cross? Where is the God of the empty tomb? Where is the God of the teacher of the Sermon on the Mount? Where is the God who speaks one word to the dead: *"Arise"*? Where is the God who speaks but one word to the lame: *"Walk"*? Where is the God of the mountain, who has but one word for his disciples: *"Go"*? Where is the God of the boat on the raging sea, with his word: *"Be still"*?

God help us when we finally meet him. And every knee bows and every tongue is shamed into silence, and we can only see the blinding light of the throne. And there he sits, the Creator God, the maker of heaven and earth. There he sits, on the interface of time and eternity. There he sits, ready to judge the quick and the dead! There he sits... Yahweh is his Name.

Be silent, be silent. A whisper is
   heard.
Be silent and listen, treasure each
   word!
Tread softly, tread softly, the Master
   is here.
Tread softly, tread softly, He bids us
   draw near.

Loganville Christian Church
April 18, 2010

Invocation

God of the ages, God of the season, God of this day,
God of this morning…be with us still.
God of the galaxies, God of the stars, God of the sun and the moon…be with us still.
God of all beauty, God of all music, God of all poetry…
be with us still.
God of all caring, God of all hope, God of all laughter,
God of all love…be with us still!
For our prayer is made in the Savior's name,
Amen.

Pastoral Prayer

All-holy and all-loving God, our prayers this day are for thy suffering children all around the world. Volcanoes and earthquakes and hunger and disease and warfare and senseless cruelty abound and love is no longer their solace.

Come, Lord Jesus, come!
Let your presence be our comfort. Let your promises be
our hope. Let your love be our guide and our goal.
Let heaven be our future and our fortune. Let praise be
our daily joy, and our service its own reward.

We pray for our sick. We pray for our discouraged,
We pray for all who have lost hope.
We pray for all with disturbed children.
We pray for all who are becoming parents for their
    parents.
Hear our prayers for they are made in the name of
    him who taught us when we pray to say
(The Lord's Prayer)

Loganville Christian Church
April 25, 2010

Prayers

Invocation

All-loving and all-patient God, ennoble our worship with your presence, for our focus this day is praise. Every hymn, every prayer, every Bible passage is wrapped up in praise. The sermon is a statement of praise.

As we lift our voices, let your strong name lift our souls—lift our praise to the throne of heaven. It is our wish, our longing, and our prayer.

Through Jesus Christ our Lord—Amen.

Pastoral Prayer

Into our hearts, into our hearts;
Come into our hearts, Lord Jesus.
Come in today, Come in to stay.

Come into our hearts, Lord Jesus.

Lord, the world can be so cold and dark. We are not brave enough to challenge the cold and the dark nor strong enough. So come, Lord Jesus, come. Minister to this congregation as thou dost see fit. The sick need thy presence, and so do the lonely and depressed. Our nation languishes—lost in the byways of greed and pleasure and the love of power.

And our congregation needs your strength and leadership.

Hear our prayers, for they are made in the name of him who taught us when we pray to say:
(The Lord's Prayer)

North Clarendon Baptist Church
2012–2013

September 9. 2012
Pastoral Prayer

All-loving and all-gracious and all-forgiving God, accept our prayers this day. Our prayers are, first of all, for our country. God bless America, Lord, God bless America! We so desperately need your blessing, but we deserve it not at all. Discord and deceit rule us, and so much of our culture is an embarrassment. We have let "Is it legal?" replace "Is it right?" in our lexicon of values.

Dear God, forgive us...forgive our foolish ways. Give us penitent hearts and contrite spirits. Focus our lives on helping others. Make us sensitive to the needs of those around us who are less fortunate than we are.

Heal the sick where you can.

Bless the hungry and the lonely.

Guide the wandering home.

Give all of us patience in helping those who have lost their way.

Bless our pastor. Show us how we can be a blessing to him.

Now guide us to the straight path with the narrow gate that will lead us home. Give us cheerful hearts on our journey and a song to brighten each day.

For we make our prayer in the name of Him who taught us, when we pray, to say:
Our Father.

North Clarendon Baptist Church, Scottsdale, Georgia
September 9, 2012

A Meditation

And It Was Night
John 13:21–30

It was supper time for what was to be the group's Last Supper. Some sacred, even holy, things were to be said and done—sacred things that became the foundation for Holy Communion, a two-thousand-year-old tradition that has been a blessing for millions around the world; sacred things not to be defamed by the presence of such as Judas Iscariot.

So Jesus told him to leave. "Go about your business." And he did. Up and out the door and hurrying down the street toward the Temple. Can you hear him running? The slap of his sandals on the cobblestone street. He is running toward the priests and Pharisees, running toward the money, running toward his destiny, running toward a rope and the creaking limb of an old tree. He is running toward darkness!

And it was night! Oh yes, it was surely night. Night because the sun had gone down; night because the forces of evil were gathering for their assault on all righteousness, an assault that was to begin this very night, even before the cock crows in the morning. Black, stygian night. The moon and stars could make no dent in that darkness. Judas left, and it was night.

The use of light and darkness to symbolize good and evil has been around for thousands of years. I guess, in just about every culture. The Jews and Christians certainly have both used light to symbolize Good. In one place, God is referred to as light. "God is light, and in him is no darkness at all" (1 John 1:05). On the other hand, darkness represents evil. In one place, hell is said to be "outer darkness." Both images are used many times, and both are impressed on our minds.

Except—except it is not always so. I have now come to believe that there is a very good side to darkness. Darkness can be very useful, very beneficial. We need darkness. We need darkness for the natural rhythms of our bodies and of our lives. We need darkness for rest.

And God needs darkness, too. God needs darkness for a screen. Whenever God needs to do something, something that is too sacred for our prying, profane eyes, God wraps the event in darkness. God uses the darkness as a curtain. Look at the text and see:

The savior of the world was to be born. To all outward signs, it was to be a normal human birth. But it was not normal! This was the coming of God to all humankind for the salvation of the world. Now, there is a sense in which all births are sacred and mysterious and holy, but this one will happen on a higher scale. This was to be God's own son! It was an event of epic proportions, cosmically significant. So God shielded it from the casually curious by wrapping the scene in darkness. As the babe was wrapped in swaddling clothes, so the night wrapped all in its embrace.

And again, the Savior of the world was to die, crucified, naked, screaming in pain. The picture became too painful—too painful, even for God. So God turned out the lights. Darkness descended, and Jesus was at least spared the final indignity of the mocking gaze and laughter of the celebrating crowd. Three hours of blessed darkness, and when the light returned, Jesus was gone. A bloody body was left, but Jesus gone. It was the middle of the day, but at God's command, it was night.

And again, the Savior of the world is to be gloriously raised from the dead. The cosmos quake as death and hell break open. Look. Look. He comes. No. No looking. He comes, all right, and death and hell will never be the same. But no one sees it happen! No one sees the first tremble of the prostrate form. No one sees the swaddling clothes of death cast off. No one sees the stone roiled away. It all happens at night. Too sacred for human eyes. In the morning, Mary and Peter and John will come. Mary will actually meet the risen Christ. But no one saw the resurrection. It happened at night.

These sacred miracles changed the history of our world—the birth, death, and resurrection of our Lord. In each instance, God used darkness as the venue for the miracle. God still works miracles in our world and in our lives. Strange as it may seem, darkness is still the preferred environment.

How often is it that grace is poured out on us—measure beyond measure—when we are experiencing our darkest times? Our night, our "dark night of the soul" is God's opportunity for miracles. Are you "feeling tough" right now? More than just "feeling tough," is the darkness covering you like a blanket so that you can't breathe? Is an illness sapping the life right out of you? Has a recent death of a friend or the recent death of a marriage or the recent death of a child or the recent death of a love relationship has life eaten a hole in your heart so that your faith has drained away? Are you ashamed to let even your church family know how bad it is? Are you afraid that they wouldn't understand? Are you afraid that the preacher wouldn't understand? Are you alone in knowing the burden, the guilt, and the tears of depression? You alone. Alone before fate. Alone before the endless empty years. Alone before death. Alone before God! Alone in the darkness... the hated darkness.

Look up. Raise your head and open your eyes! When your darkness is the deepest is when God does the best work. When it is midnight in your life, look up. God is getting ready to work a miracle in you. It might not be the miracle you want. The loved one you have prayed for might not get well. You might not get well, but a miracle will be yours— the miracle of the presence of the risen Christ.

The Psalmist says, "Yea, though I walk through the valley of the shadow of death, I will fear no evil, for thou art with me." The Psalmist doesn't say that God will help us avoid going through that valley— we all must! What is promised is that we will not have to go through that valley of death alone. The sure miracle—God's comfort—is God's presence. When the darkness is the most oppressive, listen for the still, small voice.

God's miracle will usually come in the form of a friend or a family member. God's strength and grace are usually channeled through a loving voice, a loving touch, a loving note, a loving hug. As a friend of mine once said, "I cannot imagine love without a face."

So God puts a face on the miracles—your face and mine, your hands and mine, your voice and mine.

Make no mistake, it is God's power, God's grace, God's hope, God's miracle all channeled to us to minister to our needs and the needs of our loved ones. It is God's plan to make real God's presence! An old hymn says it best:

I've seen the lightning flashing; I've
heard the thunder roll.
I've felt sin's breakers dashing, trying
to conquer my soul.

I've heard the voice of Jesus, telling
  me still to push on.
He promised never to leave me, never
  to leave me alone
No, never alone, no never alone.
He promised never to leave me, never
  to leave me alone.
It is God's truth, this special word for
  today.
Lift up your hearts!
The Darkness flees,
See, the Day Star rises.
Dawning is at hand.

Amen.

North Clarendon Baptist Church
September 30, 2012

Call to Communion
Mephibosheth

The power and the glory of this sacred table is seen no more clearly than in the story of King Saul's grandson. His name was Mephibosheth. The story is told in 2 Samuel. King Saul is dead, and David now rules. The animosity in Saul and David's relationship has been flushed from David's mind. As a tribute to the good years, David decided to give an honor to someone in Saul's family. Most of the royal family had been killed in the war. One survived.

Jonathan's son, Mephibosheth, had not gone to war because he was a cripple—both legs injured in a childhood accident. He was alive and well, though disdained by family and friends for his injury. David heard of the young man and immediately brought him to the royal palace. There David gave him the highest honor he could. David told Mephibosheth that he wanted him to come and eat at the king's table for the rest of his life. The despised cripple had moved to the top of the social ladder.

And so it is with us. Crippled, disdained, shunted to the outer margins of society—and then we hear the "still small voice" call our name. The dark memories are pushed aside. All is forgotten, for we have been invited to join our Savior at the King's table. There, we can find strength and courage and hope for our journey.

Hear the good news!

For this hour, your name and mine is Mephibosheth. We are honored guests at the feast of God for the people of God.

North Clarendon Baptist Church
October 7, 2012

Pastoral Prayer

Into my heart, into my heart, come
into my heart
Lord Jesus. Come in today, come in
to stay, come
into my heart, Lord Jesus.

All holy and righteous God, we do indeed come into thy house this day that here, in this sacred place, you might indeed come into our hearts. Here do we seek your power and your presence and your forgiveness. Oh Lord, we need you in our hearts. Let this worship hour be for us that empowering experience we have known before.

Our prayers are prayers seeking forgiveness. Our confession is real, for our sins are real. Our prayers are also prayers of rejoicing, for we have been richly blessed. Our prayers are prayers of intercession, for we have many for whom we pray daily.

Our intercessory prayers extend to Washington and London and Moscow—to our leaders, to our soldiers, to lives sacrificed, to bodies maimed, to careers postponed—all for the love of country, our love for our native land.

For we make our prayers in the name of him who taught us, when we pray to say—

North Clarendon Baptist Church
October 21, 2012
(Loganville Christian Church, May 18, 2008)

Invocation

All-holy and all-righteous God, the week has drained our energy, used up our strength. It is to thee that we turn in our hour of need. Let this worship hour be for us, a time of energizing renewal. Let our worship be our praise. Let your spirit be our soul's guest.

Ere the ashes of the Pentecostal fires have cooled, bring us once again to the throne of grace, that in hearing thy voice our ears be opened; that in seeing thy glory, our vision be cleared. That thy glory be our joy and our hope and our mission.

Pastoral Prayer

O Lord, the heavens tell of thy glory. The sun and moon and stars by the billions tell of thy might. Even the stygian night, the eternal darkness of deep space tells of thy wonder, for even there, God is. And the whole creation says, "Amen."

So let our portion of that glory come away from the stars to our humble hearts. Of thy greatness, of thy majesty, there is no end! It is our hearts that have limits. Our needs, our emptiness cry out for that power that exceeds all expectation. Come, Holy Spirit, come, and be for us manna-water born in the rock.

Let thy presence be for the healing of our sick.

Let thy presence be for the calming of our fears.

Let thy Spirit be our guide, our comfort, our stay.

For we make our prayer in the name—

North Clarendon Baptist Church
October 28, 2012

Prayers

Invocation

All-patient and all-forgiving and all-loving God,
We enter thy house this day with praise on our lips and a song in our hearts. Glorious is thy name, O Lord, and marvelous thy judgments. Let the heavens ring with the glad news of forgiveness and steadfast love. Accept our praise, answer our prayers, and strengthen our witness, for it is all done in the Savior's name.
Amen.

Pastoral Prayer

Holy and righteous God, give ear to our prayers. Prayers for peace without gunfire, peace of mind and heart, peace with our neighbors, peace with our brothers and sisters around the world.

Hear us as we pray for an end to racism—in our town and in our world. Stiffen our spines that we become strong enough to stand shoulder to shoulder with all of our brothers and sisters in Christ.

Hear us as we pray for civility in our public discourse—for discussions without invective, for conversations without insult, for communication without cursing.

Hear us as we pray for good health, and for a quick recovery when accident and illness confront us.

Hear us as we pray for those of our extended family who are sick or discouraged or depressed or lonely or frightened. Give them the peace that passes all human understanding.

Bless our nation in this election year. Bless our leaders as they struggle with problems complex and powerful.

Keep us in the center of your will, for we make our prayer.

North Clarendon Baptist Church
November 4, 2012

Prayers

Invocation

H oly God, our prayers seek your blessings. Our hymns are our praise. Our fellowship is for our strengthening. So fill our worship as you fill our hearts. Let blessings overflow. Give us strength for our journey, even as you lighten our load.

Our prayer is made in the Savior's name. Amen.

Pastoral Prayer

Creator and Redeemer God, our prayers rise as the morning mist, bound for the throne room of heaven. Accept them as a part of our worship.

In this election season we ask your blessings on our country and our world. Let our leaders seek peace. Forgive us our corporate greed. Forgive us our incessant bent toward violence.

Bless our sick. Some have been sick a long time, some lose strength daily. Guide the doctors and nurses and support personnel.

Be with those who have suffered death and loss of possessions and loss of livelihood in the great storm of last week. The destruction surpasses description, and tears fall like the rain. Give those who have been hurt peace and hope in the dark days ahead and faith unshakeable.

For our prayer is made—

The Lord's Prayer

Our Father, who art in heaven, hallowed be thy
    name!
Thy kingdom come, thy will be done, on earth as it
    Is in heaven.
Give us this day our daily bread.
And forgive us our trespasses, as we forgive those
    who trespass against us.
And lead us not into temptation, but deliver us
    from evil,
For thine is the kingdom and the power, and the
    glory, forever.
Amen.

North Clarendon Baptist Church
November 11, 2012

Prayers

Invocation

All-patient and all-caring God, we enter thy house this day with hearts full of love—love for our fellowship, love for our extended family, love for the lost and confused and disheartened. Lord, use this hour to motivate our compassion, to focus our caring, to show us what we can do to be faithful to our calling.

Our worship is to praise thy name, O great and glorious God.

So let it be.
So let it be.
Through Christ, our living Lord.
Amen

Pastoral Prayer

O Lord, how tedious and tasteless the hour when Jesus no longer we see. For some, this hour is now. Tired and frustrated and disappointed, some can no longer enjoy life as you would have us. Some can no longer smell the flowers or hear the birds, and they are lonely. Some of them, Lord, might be in this room, in this service, today. God, be present with each one in ways only you can be. Grant them once again the joy of their salvation. Bless those who are physically ill.

Guide their doctors. We pray for our leaders. Leaders in the national government, leaders in our denomination, leaders around the world. Lead them toward peace.

Hear all our prayers, for they are made in the Savior's name, him who taught us when we pray to say:

Our Father, who art in heaven—

North Clarendon Baptist Church
November 18, 2012

Prayers

Invocation

All-loving and all-forgiving God, our prayers this day are borne on the wings of anger and desperation and fear. The pain and frustration that clouds the skies over the wreckage of superstorm Sandy will not go away. The recent election has come and gone, and it brought little change and little hope.

So come, Lord Jesus, come!
Be for us our strength and our guiding light,
For we make our prayer in the Savior's name.
Amen.

Pastoral Prayer

Speak to our hearts,
Speak to our hearts, Lord Jesus.

Come in today, come in to stay.
Come into our hearts, Lord Jesus.
Bless all sick folk everywhere.
Bless and guide everyone whose job makes them
carry a gun.
Bless those who suffer from mental illness.
Guide our political leaders, the world around.
Strengthen our family ties.
Strengthen our church family ties.
For we make our prayers in the name of Him who
taught us to pray, saying—
Our Father, who art in heaven-—

North Clarendon Baptist Church
November 25, 2012

Prayers

Invocation

All-patient and all-forgiving God, we come into thy house this day with hearts filled with thanksgiving. We have been blessed by your presence, and your power and your saving grace. On this day, thanksgiving fills our praise and directs our worship. Let our service be an acknowledgement of thy bounty.

For our prayer is made in the Savior's name, Amen!

Pastoral Prayer

Holy God, thou hast opened the windows of heaven and poured out thy blessing upon us. Let our thanksgiving be heard in the very throne room of heaven. Let our joy and our gratefulness ring out like the bells of a thousand carillons, and let every creature sing thy praise. Let the trees of the forest and the rocks of the mountainside and the crashing surf of the seven seas all give testimony to thy greatness and love.

Accept our petitions in our praise. Bless all military personnel everywhere. Bless all teachers and all students. Bless all sick children. Bless all the lonely and frightened people in hospitals and in hospice care. Forgive us all, for we make our prayers in the name of Him who taught us when we pray to say:

Our Father, who art in heaven—

November 27, 2012

Members and Friends
North Clarendon Baptist Church
Scottdale, Georgia

Dear brothers and sisters in Christ,

As many of you know, Advent is the season which begins the Christian year. It is an important time, and I want each of us to appreciate its significance.

Advent is the four-week period that precedes Christmas. It begins on the Sunday nearest November 30. It is a time of preparation, spiritual preparation for the holy season coming.

The Christian church has been observing Advent for hundreds of years, but many Protestant churches have only been introduced to this special time in the last fifty to seventy-five years.

If you have come lately to this celebration, here are a few notes to remember:

"Advent" means "coming." It is a time of preparation, of expectation, of anticipation as we await the "Advent" of our Lord. In celebrating the first

Advent, we are reminded that he promised us that he would come again—a second Advent.

The parable of the bridesmaids (Matthew 25:1–13) shows us the spirit of our observance. The bridesmaids were full of excitement at the anticipated arrival of the groom, but the story vibrates with the strong message that we must be prepared for it.

The service is filled with symbolism:

★ The wreath is a circle. It symbolizes Almighty God who has no beginning, no end.
★ The wreath is made of evergreen, symbolizing our God who is forever alive.
★ The light of the candles reminds us of Christ the Light of the world, whose Advent will light all of our lives.
★ The four candles lit sequentially show us the progress we are making toward this holy season.

The list goes on, but you get the idea. This is a glorious time in the church year, and I want each one of you to appreciate it to the depths of your heart. It is Advent! Christmas is coming! The Lord comes! The first time as a baby, the second time as King of Kings and Lord of Lords!

May this Advent season be a blessing for you and yours!

We await the Christ child!

Soli Deo Gloria

Clay Manley

Advent I Hope
Call to Celebration
Rev. Manley

Lift up your heads, O mighty gates;
behold, the glorious ruler waits!
The Sovereign One is drawing near.
The Savior of the world is here!

So come surely, Lord Jesus, as dawn follows night;
Our hearts long to greet you as roses the light.
Salvation draw near us, our vision engage.
One candle is lit for the *hope* of the age.

Scripture Lesson
Isaiah 40:1–5
Church Member

Comfort, comfort my people,
says your God.

Speak tenderly to Jerusalem, and cry to her that her warfare is ended, that her iniquity is pardoned, that she has received from the Lord's hand double for all her sins.

A voice cries: "In the wilderness, prepare the way of the Lord, make straight in the desert a highway for our God. Every valley shall be lifted up, and every mountain and hill be made low, the uneven ground shall become level, and the rough places plain.

And the glory of the Lord shall be revealed, and all flesh shall see it together, for the mouth of the Lord has spoken."

Lighting of the Candle
Church Member

Hymn of Hope
"O Come All Ye Faithful" Verse 1

O come, all ye faithful, joyful and triumphant,

O come ye, o come ye to Bethlehem.
Come and behold Him, born the
    King of angels!
O come, let us adore Him, O come
    let us adore Him, O come let us
    adore Him,
Christ, the Lord!

Advent II Peace
Call to Celebration
Rev. Manley

Μay the God of peace, who brought again from the dead our Lord Jesus, attend our worship this day. With hearts full of hope do we continue our march toward Bethlehem. May our pilgrimage renew our quest for peace. Let every part of our worship strengthen our resolve to find peace in our hearts and in our world in our time.

Come quickly, shalom, teach us how to prepare for a gift that compels us with justice to care.

Our spirits are restless 'til sin and war cease.

One candle is lit for the reign of God's peace.

Scripture Lesson
Church Member

And the peace of God, which passes all understanding, will keep your hearts and your minds in Christ Jesus. (Philippians 4:7)

Glory to God in the highest, and on earth peace among those with whom he is pleased. (Luke 2:14)

Peace I leave with you; my peace do I give to you. Let not your hearts be troubled, neither let them be afraid. (John 14:27)

Blessed are the peacemakers, for they shall be called the children of God. (Matthew 5:9)

For he is our peace, in his flesh he has made both groups into one. (Ephesians 2:14)

Lighting of the Candles
Church Member

Hymn of Peace
"O Come All Ye Faithful" Verse 2

Sing, choirs of angels, sing in
exultation,
0 sing, all ye bright hosts of heav'n
above!
Glory to God, all glory in the highest!
O come, let us adore Him,
O come, let us adore Him,
O come, let us adore Him,
Christ the Lord!

Advent III Joy
Call to Celebration
Rev. Manley

Our journey moves forward, and Bethlehem draws nigh. Soon, our quest will be fulfilled, and the babe will be for us our Lord and our light.

Come, festively sing while awaiting the birth,
Join angels in dancing from heaven to earth.

Wave banners of good news, lift high thankful praise.

One candle is lit for the joy of these days.

Pastoral Prayer

All-gracious and all-forgiving God, our day of joy is tempered by spiritual disappointment. We fail ourselves as often as we fail thee. Our cup of joy runs low, and the excitement of the Advent season has yet to reach so many.

So come, Lord Jesus, come!

We need the joy that only you can bring. Minister to us with your blessed hope. Calm us with your peace. Make Advent live in our hearts until we overflow with the good news of Bethlehem. Let the voices of the heavenly choirs thrill as no earthly choir ever can. Teach us how to dance with an angel's grace and a shepherd's excitement.

And teach us how to pray with the holy expectancy of the wise ones from afar.

For we make our prayer in the name of him who taught us when we pray to say:

> Our Father, who art in heaven, hallowed be thy name.
> Thy kingdom come, thy will be done on earth as it is in heaven.
> Give us this day our daily bread.
> And forgive us our trespasses, as we forgive those who trespass against us.
> And lead us not into temptation but deliver us from evil,
> For thine is the kingdom and the power and the glory,
> Forever.
> Amen.

Scripture Lesson
Isaiah 60:1–5a
Church Member

Arise, shine; for your light has come, and the glory of the Lord has risen upon you. For behold, darkness shall cover the earth and thick darkness the people; but the Lord will arise upon you, and his glory shall be seen upon you.

And nations shall come to your light and kings to the brightness of your rising.

Lift up your eyes round about, and see; they all gather together, they come to you; your sons shall come from afar, and your daughters shall be carried in their arms. Then shall you see and be radiant, your heart shall thrill and rejoice.

Lighting of the Candle
Church Member

Hymn of Joy
"How Great Our Joy!" Verse 4

This gift of God we'll cherish well,
That ever-joyous hearts shall fill
How great our joy! Great our joy!

Joy, joy, joy! Joy, joy, joy!
Praise we the Lord in heaven on high!
Praise we the Lord in heaven on high!

Advent IV Love
Call to Celebration
Rev. Manley

It is the fourth Sunday in Advent, and our focus on this, the last Sunday in this year's Advent season, is love. It is only fitting as love is the very heart of the Christian faith and message. The gospel is for all but most especially for the needy, for the hungry, for the lost. In a moment we will sing the third verse of "It Came upon the Midnight Clear." It calls for our compassion, our love.

> All ye, beneath life's crushing load,
> Whose forms are bending low,
> Who toil along the climbing way
> With painful steps and slow,
> Look now! for glad and golden hours
> Come swiftly on the wing:
> O rest beside the weary road,
> And hear the angels sing!

Love come alive in the needy hand, and the shared shoulder is Christ come alive every day of our journey—tenderness made real at Advent.

Scripture Lesson
Isaiah 35:1–4a
Church Member

The wilderness and the dry land shall be glad, the desert shall rejoice and blossom; like the crocus it shall blossom abundantly, and rejoice with joy and singing.

The glory of Lebanon shall be given to it, the majesty of Carmel and Sharon. They shall see the glory of the Lord, the majesty of our God.

Strengthen the weak hands, and make firm the feeble knees. Say to those who are of a fearful heart, "Be strong, fear not! Behold your God."

Lighting of the Candle
Church Member

Hymn of Love
"It Came Upon The Midnight Clear" Verse 3

All ye, beneath life's crushing load,
Whose forms are bending low,
Who toil along the climbing way
With painful steps and slow,
Look now! for glad and golden hours
Come swiftly on the wing:
O rest beside the weary road,
And hear the angels sing.

North Clarendon Baptist Church
December 2, 2012

Prayers

Pastoral Prayer

Patient and loving God, hear us as we pray. The first Advent candle is lit, and our journey toward Bethlehem has begun. Purify us on the way that we be made worthy to greet the Christ child at his birthing. Cleanse our minds, as well as our hearts cleanse our motives and our longings. Make us ready when the great day comes.

Ready to meet the Christ!
Ready to join his disciples!
Ready for service!

As you bless us, even so bless our nation, our world, and all who lead.

Bless all the sick.
Bless all the caregivers.
Bless all the lonely.

Bless the discouraged.

Bless the depressed.

For we make our prayer in the name of Him, who taught us when we pray to say:

Our Father, who are in heaven…

North Clarendon Baptist Church
December 23, 2012

Pastoral Prayer

Lord God, we gather this day to celebrate the joys of Christmas. Our focus is on family and stories and laughter. But not all is celebration, for funerals, though a part of your plan, still take away some of our joy. The catastrophe at Newtown, Connecticut, seems so close to a replaying of the slaughter of the innocents in Matthew's gospel, that we spend nights looking for reasons and consolation and meaning.

Lord, is it too much to ask when we pray for peace in our homes, our schools, our county, and our world? Too much to ask that your presence bring with it our measure of your balm from Gilead?

Lord, restore our joy.

Renew our hope.

Enliven our love

and give us *peace*.

Reassure our sick.

Be a companion for our lonely.
Forgive our negligence.
Wash away our self-centeredness.
Redeem our land.
For we make our prayer
In the name of him who taught us, when we
pray, to say:
Our Father, who art in heaven, hallowed be thy
name.
Thy kingdom come, thy will be done, on earth
as it is in heaven.
Give us this day our daily bread.
And forgive us our trespasses,
as we forgive those who trespass against us.
And lead us not into temptation, but deliver us
from evil,
For thine is the kingdom and the power and the
glory forever—
Amen.

North Clarendon Baptist Church
December 30, 2012

Prayers

Invocation

All-forgiving and all-gracious God, welcome us this day into thy presence with open arms. Crown this holiday season of feasts and hugs with the warmth only your presence brings. And we do so desperately need that warmth. For we make our prayer in the Savior's name—Amen.

Pastoral Prayer

O God of wisdom and caring, fill our worship with your presence. Without that presence, it is so easy to sink into despair. The turmoil of our nation and our world plagues us with doubt and uncertainty. Our disappointment with our nation's leaders in government and business, in education and religion, knows no bounds. Every day brings new reports of failure and immorality rewarded with bonuses and promotions. Is there no justice or integrity anywhere to be found? Oh God, let the fire fall until we have learned of righteousness and holiness and generosity and kindness.

Bless our sick folk with your presence. Bless our caregivers with your patience. Bless the sick of heart with a double portion of thy compassion.

For we make our prayers in the name of him who taught us when we pray to say:

> Our Father, who art in heaven, hallowed be thy name.
> Thy kingdom come, thy will be done, on earth as it is in heaven.
> Give us this day our daily bread.
> And forgive us our trespasses,
> as we forgive those who trespass against us.
> And lead us not into temptation, but deliver us from evil,
> For thine is the kingdom and the power and the glory forever—
> Amen.

North Clarendon Baptist Church
January 6, 2013

Prayers

Invocation

O Holy God, creator of all that is, give to our souls this blessed hour of worship. Focus our minds and hearts on thee and thy kingdom. Let prayer be our strength and our stay.

Through Jesus the Christ, our Living Lord, Amen.

Pastoral Prayer

All righteous and blessed Lord, time's page has turned, and the new year is upon us. Our journey does not start afresh, for we are burdened down with guilt left over from last year and years before that. Our sins are cumulative, and our path grows ever steeper.

So come, Lord Jesus, come!
Cleanse us of the guilt which hangs over us.
Refresh our spirits and rekindle our fires.
Make your forgiveness real once more.
Make our hope our light, and thy salvation our sure reward.
"Lead on, O King eternal, the day of march has come!"
Bless the sick.
Bless the dying.
Bless the lonely.

For we make our prayers in the name of him who taught us when we pray to say:

> Our Father, who art in heaven, hallowed be thy name.
> Thy kingdom come, thy will be done, on earth as it is in heaven.
> Give us this day our daily bread.
> And forgive us our trespasses,
> as we forgive those who trespass against us.
> And lead us not into temptation, but deliver us from evil,

For thine is the kingdom and the power and the glory forever— Amen.

North Clarendon Baptist Church
January 13, 2013

Prayers

Invocation

Keep our faces, O God, toward the coming of thy kingdom and grant us to choose thy way and not our own, that we may rest in the certainty of thy victory.

Through Jesus Christ our Lord, Amen!

Pastoral Prayer

Almighty God, there are times in our journey when your silence is frightening. There are times when the divine silence is broken by the sound of thy footsteps on our narrow road. And always, the ceaseless knocking on the door to our heart.

Reveal thyself to us, O God, in ways to match each needy heart—that in thy presence, thy light shall show us each hill to be climbed, each curve to be met. And the strength to sing our way through the narrow gate on our way to glory.

Bless those of our number who need blessing. Be patient with all of us, and, at the last day, forgive us as we enter the gates eternal.

For our prayer is made in the name of Him who taught us to pray:

> Our Father, who art in heaven, hallowed be thy name.
> Thy kingdom come, thy will be done, on earth as it is in heaven.
> Give us this day our daily bread.
> And forgive us our trespasses,
> as we forgive those who trespass against us.
> And lead us not into temptation, but deliver us from evil,
> For thine is the kingdom and the power and the glory forever—
> Amen.

North Clarendon Baptist Church
January 20, 2013

Prayers

Pastoral Prayer

Lord God,

Forgive us! We have not focused our thoughts on thee in
prayer this week. We meant to. We Just haven't had
time!

Lord God, Forgive us! We have not focused our
lives on thee

in Christian living his week. We meant to.

We just haven't had time.

Lord God, forgive us! We have not studied our
Bibles this week.

We meant to! We just haven't had time!

We've been too busy, Lord! At work, and at school,
and family chores—just busy Lord. Too busy.

Not enough rest. Not enough quiet. Not enough
    peace—
And while we were busy here and there, the week
    got away from us.

God Almighty, help us to reorder our lives.
Open our eyes to our spiritual poverty.
Open our eyes to the new day dawning.
Let that light flood the Eastern sky with
dawning from horizon to horizon!
Come into our hearts, Lord Jesus.

For we make our prayers in the name of him
who taught us when we pray to say:

> Our Father, who art in heaven, hal-
>   lowed be thy name.
> Thy kingdom come, thy will be
>   done, on earth as it is in heaven.
> Give us this day our daily bread.
> And forgive us our trespasses,
> as we forgive those who trespass
>   against us.
> And lead us not into temptation, but
>   deliver us from evil,

For thine is the kingdom, and the power, and the glory, Forever—Amen.

North Clarendon Baptist Church
February 3, 2013

Prayers

Invocation

Silently now we would open our hearts to thy presence.
That presence which is our hope, our joy, and our salvation.
Teach us to show mercy, as thou art merciful.
Teach us to show patience, as thou art patient.
Teach us to live in love, as thou art loving.
Our prayer is made to him that is born
Jesus of Nazareth, the Christ and our Lord.
Amen.

Pastoral Prayer

We make our prayers day by day and impatiently await thy voice. It is so hard to be patient and understanding when it is God on whom we call! We so want to hear thy voice, to feel thy presence, and we want it now. Our better selves know that your time is not our time, but our time is flying away, and it seems that darkness falls all around us.

If it be in thy good pleasure, come quickly, Lord; come in this hour, come today.

Bring healing on thy wings, and courage in thy grasp.

Redeem everyone who calls, and let thy loving arms be our home 'til "the roll is call up yonder," and we can call heaven our home for eternity. Our trembling prayer is made in the name of him who taught us to pray, saying:

> Our Father, who art in heaven, hallowed be thy name.
> Thy kingdom come, thy will be done, on earth as it is in heaven.
> Give us this day our daily bread.
> And forgive us our trespasses,
> as we forgive those who trespass against us.
> And lead us not into temptation, but deliver us from evil,

For thine is the kingdom and the
  power and the glory forever—
Amen.

North Clarendon Baptist Church
February 10, 2013

Prayers

Invocation

All-righteous and all-merciful God, we come into thy house this day with songs and prayers of thanksgiving and hearts of Joy. Our sins, which are many, are all washed away. Our gratitude knows no bounds. So accept our praise and our songs and our prayers. Forgive us as needed. Chastise us in our backsliding ways. Remind us of your grace, and we will not forget to praise thy name forever. Through Christ our Lord. Amen.

Pastoral Prayer

Lord God, thou who hast been for us light, and breath, and food and laughter for our needy souls, bless us still: turn our blessings into prayers for others.

We pray for those who need thee, but do not know it.

We pray for those who think themselves self-sufficient.

They walk a hard road, and lonely.

Most of all Lord, we pray for ourselves...those of us here gathered to worship. With unconfessed sin, and unacknowledged need, and unexpressed joy, we have dared to come into thy presence, even dared to see thy face.

Forgive our presumptive foolishness. Protect us from ourselves. At day's end, forgive.

For we make our prayers in the name of him who taught us when we pray, to say:

> Our Father, who art in heaven, hallowed be thy name.
> Thy kingdom come, Thy will be done, on earth as it is in heaven.
> Give us this day our daily bread.

And forgive us our trespasses,
as we forgive those who trespass
against us.
And lead us not into temptation, but
deliver us from evil,
For thine is the kingdom, and the
power, and the glory, Forever—
Amen.

North Clarendon Baptist Church
February 17, 2013

Prayers

Invocation

Cleanse us, O God, from all that frightens us,
from all that feeds our sleepless nights, from
all the littleness that casts such big
shadows on our pilgrim way.
Cleanse and chastise and soothe and heal…
For we make our prayer in the Savior's name
Amen.

Pastoral Prayer

Holy and righteous God,
The cold winds still blow, and our souls are
sometimes
chilled to the marrow. We seek warm comfort, and
all too often, we find it not at all. Springtime seems

an illusion, a mirage of the spirit.

So come, Lord Jesus, come.
Give us a foretaste of the warm loving arms which wait to
carry us across the River Jordan to a land which is fairer than day.

Renew and strengthen us on our journey, with manna enough and more, with water for our baptizing, and for our thirsty souls. Guide us around the swamps of depression and the acid burns of foolish anger. Lead us not by hand but by heart, and we will not fail to sing thy praise now and forever...
For we make our prayers in the Savior's name. Amen.

North Clarendon Baptist Church
March 3, 2013

Prayers

Invocation

All patient and forgiving God, we gather in thy house, painfully aware of our sin which so easily besets us painfully aware of our guilt. In this Lenten season, lead us to the Cross, and there let your love wash us clean. Let your grace make us whole.

Come, Lord Jesus, and redeem us, is our prayer for Jesus's sake—Amen.

Pastoral Prayer

Open my eyes that I may see
Glimpses of truth thou hast for me.
Place in my hands the wonderful key
That shall unclasp and set us free.

Silently now we wait for thee.
Ready, O God thy will to see.
Open my eyes, illumine me.
Spirit divine!

Open our eyes to the pain around us—the hunger, the cold, the sickness, the violence. Open our souls to the pain within us the fear, the anger, the hopelessness, the futility, the sadness. We need so much, give us one thing more a double portion of your forgiving love. For we make our prayers in the name of him who taught us when we pray to say:

> Our Father, who art in heaven, hallowed be thy name.
> Thy kingdom come, thy will be done, on earth as it is in heaven.
> Give us this day our dally bread.
> And forgive us our trespasses,
> as we forgive those who trespass against us.
> And lead us not into temptation, but deliver us from evil,
> For thine is the kingdom and the power and the glory forever—
> Amen.

North Clarendon Baptist Church
March 10, 2013

Prayers

Invocation

All holy and righteous God, heavenly creatures circle thy throne singing songs of praise:
"Holy, holy, holy Lord God of hosts."

Heaven is filled up with glory and thanksgiving and adoration and awe and song.
All-loving and patient God, we would join those voices of praise. Let our worship be lifted up 'til it joins the swelling chorus, and we are lost in the choirs of heaven.

Let it be Lord, for this hour, let it be.
For Jesus's sake, Amen

Pastoral Prayer

> "I have been driven many times to my knees by the overwhelming conviction that I had nowhere else to go" (Abraham Lincoln).

Let us pray.

Loving God, whom we dare call Father, hear us as we pray:
Hear our prayers of thanksgiving.
We have been so blessed by your presence.
Hear our prayers of confession.
Our sins are many, our memory is short.
Hear our prayers of petition.
Some are so sick. Some are just sick of being sick.
Hear our prayers of hope.
Help us to rest easy as we face our uncertain future.
Hear our prayers for the world's leaders.
Hear our prayers for the military forces that they command.
Hear our prayers for all doctors and nurses and caregivers.
Hear our prayers for retired folk everywhere.
Hear our prayers for the lost.

Hear our prayers for the depressed.
Hear our prayers for the angry.
Hear our prayers for the hungry.
Hear our prayers for those who are afraid of dying.
So many needs. O God of love, minister to us as thou dost see fit.

For we make our prayers in the name of Jesus our Lord, him who taught us when we pray to say:

> Our Father, who art in heaven, hallowed be thy name.
> Thy kingdom come, thy will be done, on earth as it is in heaven.
> Give us this day our daily bread.
> And forgive us our trespasses,
> as we forgive those who trespass against us.
> And lead us not into temptation, but deliver us from evil,
> For thine is the kingdom and the power and the glory forever—
> Amen.

North Clarendon Baptist Church
March 17, 2013

Prayers

Invocation

All-loving and all-forgiving God, we enter thy house this day with joy and thanksgiving. Your blessings have been a measure of your love and not our doing. Our joy is a reflection of that compassion, and we can do naught but respond in worship that is filled with adoration and praise. So accept our prayers, our singing, and our preaching. For it is all offered in the Savior's name.

Amen.

Pastoral Prayer

All-wise and all-compassionate God, we lift our souls to thy throne of grace in confession and contrition. The Lenten season draws to a close, and we have not spent much time on our knees in prayer. We have not served thee as we ought. We have not been present for the needy nor served the least of these.

Our prayers of contrition seem hollow when judged by our actions, and hypocrisy is close at hand. Forgive us Lord! Enliven us to our tasks, and make our shortcomings a constant reminder of opportunities for service left untouched by the wayside. Bless our world! Bless our leaders. Bless the new Pope. Fill him with inspired wisdom. Give us all a passion for peace. Speak tenderly to the lost. Redeem us by thy power. For we make our prayer in the name of him who taught us when we pray to say:

> Our Father, who art in heaven, hallowed be thy name.
> Thy kingdom come, thy will be done, on earth as it is in heaven.
> Give us this day our daily bread.
> And forgive us our trespasses,
> as we forgive those who trespass against us.
> And lead us not into temptation, but deliver us from evil,
> For thine is the kingdom and the power and the glory forever—
> Amen.

North Clarendon Baptist Church
Palm Sunday
March 24, 2013

Prayers

Invocation

All-glorious God, we do enter thy house this Palm Sunday with songs and shouts and laughter and Palm branches. Let the glory of this day be ours. Fill our hearts to overflowing with divine joy. Let celebration rule. And we will praise thy name forever.

In Christ's name we pray.

Amen.

Pastoral Prayer

Loving God,
Some days, the weather holds the promise of spring.
Some days, it seems that winter will last forever.
And the weather mirrors our souls.

In all our days, dear Lord, whatever they be, our
need for thee is unchanging. And that need
pulls us to thee.

O Lord, do not hold back!

Let thy loving arms enfold us. Be not far from us.
Hold us dear, and we will not cease our songs of
praise and shouts of joy.

Hear our prayers; accept our service to the kingdom. Heal our sick, and renew our church.

For our prayer is made in the name of Him who
taught us, when we pray to say:

> Our Father, who art in heaven, hal-
> lowed be thy name.
> Thy kingdom come, thy will be
> done, on earth as it is in heaven.
> Give us this day our daily bread.
> And forgive us our trespasses,
> as we forgive those who trespass
> against us.
> And lead us not into temptation, but
> deliver us from evil.
> For thine is the kingdom and the
> power and the glory forever—
> Amen.

North Clarendon Baptist Church
March 31, 2013
(See also April 8, 2007)

Prayers

Invocation

All glory and honor be to thee, our risen and reigning Lord! With joyful hearts do we welcome thee this Easter Day. With songs and prayers do we lift our praise to thy throne room in heaven. Now accept our worship, hear our thanksgiving, hear our confession, bless our offering.

Accept us! For we make our prayers in the Risen Savior's name, Amen.

Pastoral Prayer

O thou who dost know us altogether and who loves us still, welcome us to thy throne room with your warm embrace. Our hearts are, this day, full of gratitude and thanksgiving. Easter is our annual reminder of all that you have done for us, most especially in the sending of your son to us—our Savior, Redeemer, and Lord. Let his coming to Earth make of us light for this darkened world and salt for the decaying world. Use us for the blessing we were meant to be. Make our lives our response to thy divine Easter gift. Our failures are no indication of our love for thee, so cover them with thy patience and forgiveness. Lord of all, make our weakness our key to thy compassionate love.

Our prayer is made in the name of Him who taught us when we pray to say:

> Our Father, who art in heaven, hallowed be thy name.
> Thy kingdom come, thy will be done, on earth as it is in heaven.
> Give us this day our daily bread.
> And forgive us our trespasses,
> as we forgive those who trespass against us.
> And lead us not into temptation, but deliver us from evil,

For thine is the kingdom and the power and the glory forever— Amen.

North Clarendon Baptist Church
April 7, 2013

Prayers

Invocation

All-holy and all-wise God, into thy house do we come this day, seeking blessing and guidance.

We need thy love and thy understanding and thy forgiveness.

We need thy guidance and thy leadership and thy patience when we stray.

It is to thy house that we come, for we have nowhere else to turn.

Let our worship be acceptable to thee and thy response a bounty of blessing.

For we make our prayer in the Savior's name. Amen.

Pastoral Prayer

Creator God,

Hear our prayers this day. We have sick and depressed and discouraged folk in our church family. We have lonely and frightened ones as well. So much spiritual hunger. We need thy presence in power. Come, Lord Jesus, and fill our assembly with thy powerful love.

Bless all those for whom we should pray. Accept our thanks for our heroes who have given the last full measure of devotion. Hear our prayers for the families and friends of those now gone from us. Let this blessed day be for all of us a renewal of our loyalties, a renewal of our commitment, and a pledge to work for peace.

Hear our prayers, for they are made in the name of Jesus Christ, he who taught us when we pray to say:

> Our Father, who art in heaven, hallowed be thy name.
> Thy kingdom come, thy will be done, on earth as it is in heaven.
> Give us this day our daily bread.
> And forgive us our trespasses,

as we forgive those who trespass
against us.
And lead us not into temptation, but
deliver us from evil,
For thine is the kingdom and the
power and the glory forever—
Amen.

North Clarendon Baptist Church
April 14, 2013

Prayers

Invocation

All-loving and all-forgiving God, we have come to thy house this day seeking thy blessing. We need love, and we need hope. We need understanding, and we need forgiveness. So bless us as you will. Guide us when we wander. Save us from ourselves.

May this time of worship be enriched by your presence, for we make our prayer in the Savior's name. Amen!

Pastoral Prayer

God of the Bible, God of prayer, God of the saints, hear us as we pray.

Some of our congregation are discouraged, some are frightened, and some are lonely. Help them each and every one.

Some of our congregation are full of joy and seek out the dark places on the back streets to carry their message of love. Thank you God for these souls who set the pace for service. Some of our number are sick…sick with disease, with accident, with old age.

Lord, if it be in thy good pleasure, speak tenderly to each one. Crack the windows of heaven as we join St. Paul in a brief glimpse of the glory that awaits. Clear away the "darkened glass," that the morning rays be not bent or hindered or clouded over.

Our prayer is made in the Savior's name, him who taught us when we pray to say:

> Our Father, who art in heaven, hallowed be thy name.
> Thy kingdom come, thy will be done, on earth as it is in heaven.
> Give us this day our daily bread.
> And forgive us our trespasses,
> as we forgive those who trespass against us.

And lead us not into temptation, but
    deliver us from evil,
For thine is the kingdom and the
    power and the glory forever—
Amen.

North Clarendon Baptist Church
April 21, 2013

Prayers

Invocation

All holy and righteous God, it is with bowed heads and reverent hearts that we enter thy house this day. We know that we dare not demand thy presence. We are unworthy of such, so we beg for it. Open the doors of heaven that our prayers may be heard. Open the doors of our hearts that our confession may be heard. Prepare us for your feast, for we make our prayer in Jesus's name…

Amen.

Pastoral Prayer

Gracious God, Creator God, hear us as we:
Pray for others! We pray for all who carry a gun.
We pray for all who carry a book.

We pray for all who carry a stethoscope.
We pray for all who care for babies.
We pray for all who teach children.
Hear us as we:
Pray for ourselves!
Some of us have been sick for so long.
Some have been lonely for so long.
Bless our church, for there is so much to do, and so
few to do it. Strengthen our resolve. Point us to
a new day aborning.

Hear us as we:

Pray for our leaders!
For all leaders do we pray for wisdom and kindness, for integrity, for honesty, for commitment, for
energy, for dedication to the cause.

For we make our prayer in the name of him
who taught us when we pray to say:

Our Father, who art in heaven, hallowed be thy name.
Thy kingdom come, thy will be
done, on earth as it is in heaven.
Give us this day our daily bread.

And forgive us our trespasses,
as we forgive those who trespass
against us.
And lead us not into temptation, but
deliver us from evil,
For thine is the kingdom and the
power and the glory forever—
Amen.

North Clarendon Baptist Church
April 28, 2013

Prayers

Invocation

All holy and righteous God, we do enter thy house this day with troubled hearts. So many institutions, so many officials and leaders have let us down. Their integrity has proven empty.

Our fears and anxieties are strengthened as terror and terrorism now stalk our shores.

Lord God, make this worship hour a time of renewal and empowerment and courage, all for the facing of these troubled times. For we make our prayer in the Savior's name, Amen.

Pastoral Prayer

Lord God, you made us in your likeness and promised to be with us day to day, summer and winter, seed time and harvest, and it has been so.

On that reliability do we depend this day. We need thee, desperately need thee every hour, every day. The rocks with which we build have turned to sand. Strength and power have been lost, and there seems to be nothing on which we can depend.

Bless us, Lord, and save us. Keep us sheltered in thy bosom until Jesus comes.

Bless our sick. Bless the lonely. Bless the despondent. Bless the depressed.

For we make our prayers in the name of him who taught us when we pray to say:

> Our Father, who art in heaven, hallowed be thy name.
> Thy kingdom come, thy will be done, on earth as it is in heaven.
> Give us this day our daily bread.
> And forgive us our trespasses,
> as we forgive those who trespass against us.
> And lead us not into temptation, but deliver us from evil,
> For thine is the kingdom and the power and the glory forever—
> Amen.

North Clarendon Baptist Church
May 5, 2013

Prayers

Invocation

Into thy house do we come this day with praise in our hearts and a song to be sung. Glorious is thy name, O Lord, and marvelous thy judgments. All glory and honor be to thee, and let the heavens ring out the glad news forever and ever—for our prayer is made in the Savior's name. Amen.

Pastoral Prayer

All holy and all righteous God, there is much for which to pray. In this time of worship, our prayers rise to the heavens, claiming your promises for peace.
Peace from gunfire,
Peace of mind and heart,

Peace with our neighbors,
Peace around the world.

As we are caught up in daily living, hear our prayers for civility,

for discussion without invective,

for conversation without cursing,

for disagreement without anger.

Lord, we are hemmed in, and we long to be set free. Our bodies and our minds and our souls all feel entangled in the world, and it is strangling us beyond redemption. So come, Lord Jesus, come. Liberate us from the sins which so easily beset us. If it be in your will, heal us in all the ways you can. Guide us toward the light. Lift us when we fall. Give us caring hearts, for we make our prayers in the name of him who taught when we pray to say:

> Our Father, who art in heaven, hallowed be thy name.
> Thy kingdom come, thy will be done, on earth as It is in heaven.
> Give us this day our daily bread.
> And forgive us our trespasses,
> as we forgive those who trespass against us.

And lead us not into temptation, but
deliver us from evil,
For thine is the kingdom and
the power and the glory
forever—Amen.

North Clarendon Baptist Church
May 12, 2013

Prayers

Invocation

All holy and patient God, the miracle of spring is glorious, and it puts a song In our hearts. But the miracle of spring is fleeting, and so is our drift toward summer. Make us sensitive, Lord, to nature's lessons. Your grandeur is unchanging, but your flowers will fade by nightfall. Teach us how to move with the seasons and how to number our days. Soften the pain of our days' passing with thy fellowship even as we walk through our garden in the cool of the evening.

Guide us for Jesus's sake, Amen.

Pastoral Prayer

Lord God, our prayer is for the sick and the suffering. Bless and heal them is our prayer. Our prayer is for our leaders—all leaders of nations both great and small. Teach them how to solve problems without guns and bombs. And every solution need not be stained by blood. If it be in thy good pleasure, ease the stress of everyday living, that we be not inundated by anger and frustration and subliminal fear.

Lord God. We need so much! Our prayers often seem to be incoherent babbling, for we have much to ask. Even we are confused by the multiple needs of our wayward souls. So hasten thy coming, dear Lord, ere we perish.

Our prayer is made in the name of him who taught us when we pray to say:

> Our Father, who art in heaven, hallowed be thy name.
> Thy kingdom come, thy will be done, on earth as it is in heaven.
> Give us this day our daily bread.
> And forgive us our trespasses,

as we forgive those who trespass
against us.
And lead us not into temptation, but
deliver us from evil,
For thine is the kingdom and the
power and the glory forever—
Amen.

North Clarendon Baptist Church
May 19, 2013

Prayers

Invocation

O God of comfort, O God of challenge, O God of spirit wind and spirit fire, we have come here this day seeking that promised comfort, that promised challenge, and that promised fire. So accept our worship! Make it a time of celebration and praise.

Let thy voice again be heard! Let the flames descend!

Our prayer is made in the Savior's name, Amen!

Pastoral Prayer

All Holy God, in millennia past thou didst let thy Spirit move across our land, through our churches, in our homes, in our hearts. Our prayer this day is that you might do it again. In the power of thy Spirit, enrich our worship, enliven our witness, and flood our souls with saving grace.

Our sick need thy comfort. Dr. Ginn's family needs reassurance and strength. So many of our friends and members are lonely and frightened. Some are in pain. Some are worried about parents, some about grandchildren. Whatever the need, be present in love.

For we make our prayers in the name of him who taught us when we pray to say:

> Our Father, who art in heaven, hallowed be thy name.
> Thy kingdom come, thy will be done, on earth as it is in heaven.
> Give us this day our daily bread.
> And forgive us our trespasses,
> As we forgive those who trespass against us.
> And lead us not into temptation, but deliver us from evil,
> For thine is the kingdom and the power and the glory forever—
> Amen.

North Clarendon Baptist Church
May 26, 2013

Prayers

Invocation

Holy and righteous God, be gentle with our memories this special day. Memorial Day has a sacred place in our corporate lives—a day of honor, a day of respect, a day of respect, a day of thanksgiving. All of these emotions and more stir us in powerful ways, stir us to song and stir us to tears.

So come, Lord Jesus, come.

Bless our worship with your presence, as our praise finds voice in silence and in songs and in sermon. For our prayer is made in the Savior's name. Amen.

Pastor's Prayer

Ask for people who have lost loved ones in military combat.

Ask for people who have family members now serving in the military.

O God of peace, hear our prayers for peace on this Memorial Day. Hear our prayers of thanksgiving for those loved ones who have sacrificed much in service to our country. Bless those who have supported our efforts to bring peace and stability to a world now trembling with uncertainty and fear.

So much of which to be proud.

So much for which we need forgiveness.

So much work to be done.

Help us in helping others, is our prayer.

We pray for the grieving folk of Moore, Oklahoma. The devastation of their homes is only matched by the devastation of their souls. We pray for our church, for our sick, for our government, for our denomination, for our families in distress.

Hear our prayers, for they are made in the name of him who taught us when we pray to say:

Our Father, who art in heaven, hallowed be thy name.

Thy kingdom come, thy will be done, on earth as it is in heaven.

Give us this day our daily bread.

And forgive us our trespasses, as we forgive those who trespass against us.

And lead us not into temptation, but deliver us from evil,

For thine is the kingdom and the power and the glory forever—

Amen.

North Clarendon Baptist Church
July 7, 2013

Prayers

Invocation

O God of peace and light and sunsets and roses,
In humility do we enter thy house.
We have sins to confess, and victories to share,
and joys for each one.
Enrich our worship with your presence,
For our prayer is made in the Savior's name—
Amen.

Pastoral Prayer

All-holy, and all-wise, and all-loving God,
We have gathered here this day because we need to.
We need thy powerful presence.
We need thy forgiveness. We need thy compassion.
We need to relax spiritual ly in thy loving arms.

So teach us how to be grateful/
Teach us how to be faithful.
Teach us how to be loyal.
Teach us how to be quiet.
When it is possible, heal.
When it is possible, forgive.
As it is possible, save.

All glory and honor be to thee, O God, our guard and guide and stay! Our task and privilege this day is to worship thee.

So come, Lord Jesus, and take us all to thy bosom. Point us to our appointed tasks, and we will not forget to sing thy praises forever and beyond forever into eternity.

For we make our prayers in the name of him who taught us when we pray to say:

> Our Father, who art in heaven, hallowed be thy name.
> Thy kingdom come, thy will be done, on earth as it is in heaven.
> Give us this day our daily bread.
> And forgive us our trespasses,

as we forgive those who trespass
  against us.
And lead us not into temptation, but
  deliver us from evil,
For thine is the kingdom and the
  power and the glory forever—

North Clarendon Baptist Church
July 14, 2013

Prayers

Invocation

All glory and honor be to thee, O God, our guard and guide and stay!

Our task and privilege this day is to worship thee.

So come, Lord Jesus, and take us all to thy bosom. Point us to our appointed task, and we will not forget to sing thy praises forever and beyond forever into eternity.

Through Christ, our Lord, Amen.

Pastoral Prayer

Hear our prayers, O Lord, as we bow our heads and hearts.

Hear our prayers, even as they rise to the skies and reach the throne room of heaven.

Hear them, O God, in love and patience. We know that our prayers are often self-centered, but we cannot help it. Our prayers are like they are because we are like we are. So bless us Lord, in kindness, bless us.

Hear our prayers for our church!

Hear our prayers for our extended church family!

Hear our prayers for our nation!

Hear our prayers for all military personnel.

Hear our prayers for all school teachers—elementary school, high school, and college.

For we make our prayers in the name of him who taught us when we pray to say:

> Our Father, who art in heaven, hallowed be thy name.
> Thy kingdom come, thy will be done, on earth as it is in heaven.
> Give us this day our daily bread.
> And forgive us our trespasses,
> as we forgive those who trespass against us.

And lead us not into temptation, but
    deliver us from evil,
For thine is the kingdom and the
    power and the glory forever—
Amen.

North Clarendon Baptist Church
July 21, 2013

Prayers

Invocation

All loving God, our prayer is a hymn.
"O tell us of his might, O sing of his grace whose
    robe is the light, whose canopy space."
So we lift our voices in praise to thee, O Most High.
We will tell of his might;
We will sing of his grace.
In awesome wonder, we will declare the light from
    the sun to be his robe and his canopy is space.
How awesome is our God, how wondrous, how
    loving!
Accept our worship, O God, for it is made in the
    Savior's name.
Amen.

Pastoral Prayer

Gracious and forgiving God, our burdens are weighing us to the ground. The forces of nature plague us with summer's heat which is beyond our bearing, with fires that sweep away forests and homes into smoke and ashes. Tornadoes and floods destroy all in their path, and we feel helpless. We can only bury the dead and weep. Love us through the pain. Wipe our eyes that we may once again see the vision that awaits us beyond our thin horizon. And give us strength to push on and push up 'til thy throne room in glory is our place in glory...for we make our prayers in the name of him who taught us when we pray to say:

> Our Father, who art in heaven, hallowed be thy name.
> Thy kingdom come, thy will be done, on earth as it is in heaven.
> Give us this day our daily bread.
> And forgive us our trespasses,
> as we forgive those who trespass against us.
> And lead us not into temptation, but deliver us from evil,
> For thine is the kingdom and the power and the glory forever—
> Amen.

North Clarendon Baptist Church
July 28, 2013

Prayers

Invocation

O Holy God, creator and sustainer of all that is, give us this hour of sacred time. Focus our worship on thee and thy kingdom. Make this an hour of blessing and renewal. Our prayer is made in the Savior's name, Amen.

Pastoral Prayer

All-loving and all-forgiving God, hear our prayers for our church. We pray for each and every member and friend. Some of our number are sick, some are lonely, some are happy and blest. Bless and heal every one. Give each of us our portion of grace and peace and hope. In the strength of thy presence, bind us together in love and commitment. What we pray for ourselves do we ask for all thy children round the world.

So come, Holy Spirit, come!
Forgive and inspire and heal,

For we make our prayers in the name of Him who taught us, when we pray to say:

> Our Father, who art in heaven, hallowed be thy name.
> Thy kingdom come, thy will be done, on earth as it is in heaven.
> Give us this day our daily bread.
> And forgive us our trespasses,
> as we forgive those who trespass against us.
> And lead us not into temptation, but deliver us from evil,
> For thine is the kingdom and the power and the glory forever—
> Amen.

North Clarendon Baptist Church
August 4, 2013

Prayers

Invocation

All-righteous God, we enter thy house this day
with thankfulness in our hearts and gratitude in our
souls, for our blessings are bountiful, our lives are
enriched, and all because of your love and care.

So make our worship full of joy and reassurance
and everlasting praise.

Our prayer is made in the Savior's name. Amen.

Pastoral Prayer

Come, Lord Jesus, come! Descend on us with forgiveness and love abounding.
Such is our prayer! Such is our hope! Such is our
need!

Heal us from sin's dark stain. Free us from the shackles of hopelessness.

Loose our bonds and set us free.

Free us to honorable service in the kingdom…

Free us to the joy of blessed songs of praise…

Free us to soar on the wings of the morning…

To shout "Hosanna" until the bells of heaven lead our praise.

Heal the sick! Heal our churches! Heal our nation! Heal our world.

Bless the poor. Bless the lost. Bless all sick children everywhere. For we make our prayer in the name of him who taught us when we pray to say:

> Our Father, who art in heaven, hallowed be thy name.
> Thy kingdom come, thy will be done, on earth as it is in heaven.
> Give us this day our daily bread.
> And forgive us our trespasses,
> as we forgive those who trespass against us.
> And lead us not into temptation, but deliver us from evil.

For thine is the kingdom and the
 power and the glory forever—
Amen.

North Clarendon Baptist Church
August 11, 2013

Prayers

Invocation

God of Gods, Lord of lords, Light of lights, thou hast bid us to come into thy presence, and here we are gathered. We seek whatever thou wouldst give.

We pray that it be blessing and guidance and hope.

Our prayer is made in the Savior's name. Amen.

Pastoral Prayer

"Giver of every good and perfect gift," hear us as we pray.

Fountain of forgiveness and hope and joy, bless us with an abundance of all thy gifts, and we will praise thy name forever.

What we would pray for ourselves, do we pray for all thy children around the world.

Let thy blessings flow!
Let healing wash through our hospitals.
Let tenderness be our daily goal.
Let gentleness be our watchword.
Strengthen those who mourn.
Encourage the depressed and the discouraged.
Take all the prayers offered here today, bind them up, and send them on to the throne room on high.

For we make our prayers in the name of him who taught us when we pray to say:

> Our Father, who art in heaven, hallowed be thy name.
> Thy kingdom come, thy will be done, on earth as it is in heaven.
> Give us this day our daily bread.
> And forgive us our trespasses,
> as we forgive those who trespass against us.
> And lead us not into temptation, but deliver us from evil,
> For thine is the kingdom and the power and the glory forever—
> Amen.

Northside Drive Baptist Church

Northside Drive Baptist Church
Good Friday Service
April 2, 1999 12:30p.m.
The Second Word

The Pastoral Prayer

Holy God,

Tis Good Friday in this Easter season and time to focus our thoughts on the cross, on sacrificial love, on the wages of sin. The hour is late in this reliving of the passion of our Savior, and some of us are not ready. Not ready for the day of Good Friday and what it represents. Not ready for the night and what it remembers.

Take our worship this day, and make it our time of preparation and transformation. Get us ready. Forgive penitent hearts. Calm the anxious. Reassure the doubting. Be with the dying. Be for each of us strength and courage and hope.

Almighty God,

Thou who didst create us, and who does sustain us still.

Thou who didst love us, and who does love us still,

Renew in each of us an awareness of the depths of thy love,

Its passion, its suffering, its sacrifice.

Gracious God, lead us through Good Friday, so we will be ready for Easter.

In the name of Jesus the Christ do we make our prayers.

Amen.

Northside Drive Baptist Church
Good Friday Service
April 18, 2014

A Meditation

My God, my God, why? Why cancer? Why the Holocaust? Why fear? Why is life so often cruel? None of us are spared. The Christ leads the way. Pain knows no boundary. Who could have imagined it? Loud protestations ring empty, for at the first sign of danger, all flee. Disciples and followers—gone, literally scared to death.

My God, my God, Why?

Oh, I know! It is all explained in the Book. The Book says that God made us and everything else. He made us with wonderful abilities and with limitless egocentric demands. For all people everywhere, "I," "me," "mine" have become the most important words in any language. For each one of us yearns for a place and the right to perform.

And God said, "No."

God said, "You can't be God, I am!" And the drama in the garden leads to cosmic emptiness a great gulf fixed. It must not end this way. Outer darkness is no fit place for the redeemed or the Redeemer.

A voice must be raised. Ere we be caught in the slough of despond. A miracle is needed! Behold! The miracle is here! It stands ready to burst forth upon every generation, including this one. A voice is heard, and salvation is nigh. Our pain has been caught up in Jesus's pain. The burden he bears is so horrific that even God turns away, and Jesus is left to scream alone, bearing your sins and mine.

And yet, even in the blackest pits of hell, a trembling was felt that day. The rocks split and the ground shook and people cried out in fear. "Fear not!" said the angels, "for a new age is aborning, and on its banner only one word in large block letters: *atonement*. Fear and pain will be banished when we are *at one* with God. Look and listen: atonement's work has already begun.

"Surely, He has borne our guilt and covered our sorrow...

All we, like sheep, have gone astray...

And the Lord has laid on Him the iniquity of us all!"

That is atonement at work, and the day star rises to meet this new day.

For some, the pain is still real. Some have not yet claimed their place in the angel's choir nor joined the legions marching to Zion. God bless them!

Some have claimed their heritage. They have renewed their faith and they soar on eagles' wings. God bless them!

Others live in a spiritual fantasy. They go through life wrapped in a cloak of certainty. They are inspired and sustained by ignorance and inexplicable confidence. God bless them!

And some find themselves—maybe only once a year—at the foot of the cross. Too desperate to run away, too needy to survive alone, trapped on a lonely hill wondering how it had come to this—a Savior dying, alone, on an old rugged cross. God bless them!

We gather on a hillside across the way. We are too embarrassed to show our cowardice and too guilt-ridden to not cover our faces…pathetic, spiritually impotent, afraid of our own tears.

We can't take our eyes off him, and we cannot close our ears to his pleading. His call to his Father is sharper than any two-edged sword. It cuts to the quick, and we cannot escape it, for Jesus's question will not go away:

My God, my God, why?

Why now? Why us? Why me?

Why! Why! Why!

Amen.

Northside Drive Baptist Church
March 26, 2017

Prayers

Loving and forgiving God,

With humble hearts do we enter into thy presence this Lenten season. Our contrition is the more real as we approach Good Friday. We are sinners saved by grace but sinners nonetheless. We need continuing forgiveness, for in our daily lives, every day is Good Friday—every day is Easter.

Let your divine presence rule!

Cast us not away from thy presence!

Revive us again, Lord. Revive us again!

In this season of confession and penitence, hear our prayers! We know that we do not deserve your grace, but we are lost without it. We know that we do not deserve your abiding presence, but without it, we die.

So come, Lord Jesus, come!
Attend to our sick and their families.
Bless the discouraged and the frightened!
Bless the lonely and the angry!
Bless those in jail and the drug addicted!
Bless all government officials everywhere!
Give them a sharp eye and a keen sense of integrity.
We need so much, give us one thing more—a dou-
ble portion of your forgiving love.

It is the Easter season. It is a time of praise and
thanksgiving, worship and prayer.
Let the power of the season prepare us for a new
day.
Wake us up with the call of a distant trumpet!
Behold, the day star rises.
Rejoice! Emmanuel!
And again I say, "Rejoice!"

For we make our prayer in the name of him
who taught us when we pray to say:

Our Father, who art in heaven, hallowed be thy name.
Thy kingdom come, thy will be
done, on earth as it is in

heaven.

Give us this day our daily bread.

And forgive us our trespasses,

as we forgive those who trespass
against us.

And lead us not into temptation, but
deliver us from evil,

For thine is the kingdom and the
power and the glory,

Forever—

Amen.

Northside Drive Baptist Church
October 2017

Pastoral Prayer

Lord God Almighty, maker of heaven and earth,
give ear to our painful supplication.

Creator and sustainer of all we have and are,
Shower us this day with a double portion
Or your patience.

Be gentle with us, Lord!
Our minds are filled with trivia, just like our lives
And our hearts.

We long for thy presence, we need thy grace. We
    ignore humility,
and we act like tears are for the weak.

In an age of lovelessness and ugliness and anger,

Forgive us when we get upset over dust settling on
   a freshly
washed car!

In this hour of worship—singing, praying,
   preaching:
When confrontation with the Most High is devoutly
   to be sought,
forgive us when our lives are filled with concern for
   what we shall
eat and what we shall wear.
Remind us of all those things that have been put in
   their rightful
place by the risen Christ.

Drop thy still dews of quietness 'til all our strivings
   cease.
Breathe through the heat of our desire, thy coolness
   and thy
balm.
Re-clothe us in our rightful minds.

And we will glorify thy name forever and forever.
In the name of him who taught us when we pray to
   say: The Lord's Prayer

Northside Drive Baptist Church
October 15, 2017

Morning Prayer

Oh Holy One, God of peace and love,
We come into thy house this day to worship thee.

Lord God,
You have told us to come into your presence like
    little children:
Simple, guileless, honest, open.
But we don't do it because we cannot…
Too many years of fooling ourselves,
Too many years of trying to fool God.

Lord, you must accept us as we are, we can be no
    other.
With our anxieties and fears and worries about
    health and job,
uncertainty about children and parents and
    friends…

With egos fired by pride and sexuality confused
    with power,
When growing up is as frightening as growing old…
With our strange ability to separate what we do
    from who we are,
and character and integrity are often as rare as the
    song of the
turtledove…
Oh see us rush to worship, trailing clouds of care…

O Holy Master,
In the stillness of this worship hour
Drop thy still dews of quietness
'til all our strivings cease.
Take from our souls the strain and stress
And let our ordered lives confess
The beauty of thy peace.

Bless, and heal, and calm, and cleanse.
And we will rejoice as the birds of the morning
And sing thy praise forevermore.
And sing thy praise…
And sing and sing and sing.

Northside Drive Baptist Church
March 4, 2018

Pastoral Prayer

God of grace, and God of glory
On thy people pour thy power.

In weakness do we pray for strength. In solitude do we pray for community. In darkness do we pray for light. Come, Lord Jesus, and enliven us with your presence.

Some of us are so needy!
Some of us are so frightened!
Some of us are so lost!

Come, Lord Jesus, come!

Part the clouds, and let the day star show forth thy praise.

Tell us of thy light, and then let your candle set the galaxies aflame.

Let all that is praise thy name.

Speak words of hope in our silence.
Speak words of challenge to our timidity.
Speak words of blessing to the sick.
Speak words of comfort to the depressed.
Speak words of courage to those afraid to die.
Speak words of courage to those afraid to live.

Forgive us when we need it.

Lead us when we wander. Let the straight path with the narrow gate be our beacon and our strength.

Let peace be our solace, our joy, and our reward…

Peace, peace, wonderful peace
Peace, peace, peace

For our prayers are made in the Savior's name—
Even Jesus Christ—he, who taught us when we pray to say: The Lord's Prayer

Northside Drive Baptist Church
April 29, 2018
(Oakhurst Baptist Church, November 4, 1990)

Pastoral Prayer

Lord God Emanuel,
Lord of lords, Light of lights
Keeper of the sunrise beyond the darkness…
Thou fountain of hope, wellspring of joy
Thou who has given us grace abounding, and peace
In times long past…hear our prayers this day!

For in the quiet of this worship hour, we find a
    name for our
disease, and that name is loneliness.
So many from among us gone…
So many moved away, but here's the rub,
So many dead…so many dead.
Leaders and followers, workers and prayers, givers
    and keepers

And faithful…Lord God A'mighty, who among us
can walk in the footsteps of faithfulness laid down
    by the likes of
the saints of old?

O Holy Master of us all,
We call upon your boundless grace…
In the name of your Son, our Savior, Jesus of
    Nazareth,
our risen Redeemer and Lord,
Save us from the modern version of the abomina-
    tion of desolation,
and its name is loneliness:
Loneliness that strikes at night,
Loneliness that strikes us at funerals,
Loneliness that strikes us at Christmas,
Loneliness that eviscerates even the strongest.
Save us, Lord. Save us now!

And when the loneliness is finally hemmed in with
    the love,
Speak to us, in ways each of us can understand,
that we might be emboldened to step forward
and fill the ranks for those now gone.

It is now our time to lead. It is our time to serve, our
time to smile, our time to give—*our time.*

And if we be found faithful servants in our time—
One reward we ask, and that with all our hearts...

When the saints go marching in—Mary Dutton,
Tommy Clyatt, Bedford Davis, Louise Davis,
Gordon Davis, John Bell—so many others, and
a million times more.

O Lord, Let us march, too.
Shoulder to shoulder, arm-in-arm
Singing the songs of Zion into the church
triumphant.

Oh Lord, we want to be in that number
When these saints go marching in.

Grant it Lord, Let it be
Through Christ our Lord.

For we make our prayers in the name of him, who taught us when we pray to say:

> Our Father, who art in heaven, hallowed be thy name.
> Thy kingdom come, thy will be done, on earth as it is in heaven.
> Give us this day our daily bread.
> And forgive us our trespasses, as we forgive those who trespass against us.
> And lead us not into temptation, but deliver us from evil,
> For thine is the kingdom and the power and the glory forever—
> Amen.

Northside Drive Baptist Church
July 1, 2018
(From Oakhurst Baptist
Church, July 30, 1989)

Pastoral Prayer

Lord God,

Winter is a distant memory and the flowers of spring long gone.

Humidity, heat, thunder, lightning and rain and even the summer is drifting away, and we are not saved. Lord God, we are not saved…

Not saved from short-sighted ignorance.

Not saved from power hungry politicians.

Not saved from those who put money before morality and self before everything.

Lord have mercy upon us.

(Choir: Kyrie Eleison)

We are not saved from the physical and mental anguish to which our human frailty is heir.

Some of us are sick.

Some of us are angry, some desperate, some out of work, some frustrated with work, and some would give all that they have and are to avoid one more lonely night.

In all these souls with their manifold needs.

In all these bodies with their physical ills.

In this congregation with all its needs and dreams...

Christ have mercy upon us, Christ have mercy! (Choir: Christe Eleison)

The seasons fly by. The sea of life is so large, and our ship is so small. It is a billion miles to the nearest star and a billion people are hungry and a billion people are oppressed and a billion oppressing, a billion sins unacknowledged, a billion sins unconfessed.

Lord, have mercy upon us. (Choir: Kyrie Eleison)

O Holy Master,
Grant us the blessing of patience.
Grant us the blessing of courage.

Grant us the blessing of hope.
Grant us the blessing of peace.

Fill us with the strength of silence, and the power of praise.

We wait for the leadership of thy Spirit.

And our prayer is made in the name of Him whom to know is life eternal,

Even Jesus the Christ, our Lord.

Who taught us when we pray to say:

Our Father, who art in heaven…

Addendum

Addendum

I have found no place to include these devotional pieces within the body of the collected prayers. I include them because they have meant so much to me over the years. They have no order. They include:

Funerals
Poems
Wedding
Meditations

God bless their usefulness in the kingdom.

Shared Time

Originally written in 1988 in response to a private counseling session with a church member.

   It was first shared with the Oakhurst congregation July 30, 1989

So rare
So fine…is shared time!

The laughter is full, and funny.
The tears are real, and scalding.

And then—careful now, this ground is both sacred and slippery—the laughter becomes tears and the tears become laughter, and anger gets verbalized, and depression, and bitterness, and longing, and a dozen emotions run together and slosh all over the table. Makes a mess!

And in this mess—light or hope or something. How can it be? Relive pain one day and you get acid indigestion. Another day—same pain, but now shared—and wholeness happens. The king of Siam said, "It's a wonderment!" Wonderment, hell, it's a miracle...maybe a miracle of grace.

And the joy of sharing that moment was mine. And the time became a present, a gift from you to me—unwrapped, untied, but unequalled.

So rare
So fine...is shared time.

A Wedding Poem

Originally written as a part of the marriage ceremony for the wedding of Nancy Benefield and Paul Durden

June 23, 1973

Once upon a time,
When there was nothing but God,
and God was very young,
Loneliness was born,
and Loneliness stalked the Halls of Heaven.

So God made Light, with Stars and Sun…
Loneliness was not banished by Light.
Well…an Earth then,
with water and fishes,
and land and plants,
and animals to admire or play with.
But Loneliness can live in a Garden like Eden,
if a garden is all that's there.

Someone to share with was needed,

for even God needs help in fighting Loneliness.
So God made a person…
strong,
bright,
sensitive

Now God had someone to talk to, and that was fine.
Spirit touching Spirit,
Life touching Life.
But the person was "One-of-a Kind."
And "One of-a-Kind" is always neuter…
And always lonely.

The Creation was not finished
Because the Creature was not finished.
So God made its other half.

God's "Person"! One entity two parts.
Spirit touching Spirit…yes.
Life touching Life…yes.
But now Body touching Body, Warmth touching
    Warmth.
Sharing became complete.
The "Person"…neuter…
Became a Man and a Woman,
Love was born…and Loneliness died.

God saw all that had been made,
And, behold, it was very good.

The millennia since have proven God right.
People need God, and God needs people.
People need love, and God is where it comes from.
Love enters life in a thousand ways;
a Mother's breast,
a Father's hands,
a Friend's laughter.
But it is easiest to know in loving arms.

Marriage celebrates that truth,
And that is why we are here today.

God made marriage,
and if God hadn't made it,
somebody would have invented it.

Acknowledging that marriage is of God,
In what spirit shall we observe this sacred ceremony?
Let none doubt,
We are in God's Presence!
We have God's Blessing!

Therefore it is only fitting…
The wedding must begin with
Thanksgiving and Celebration!

Glory to God in the Highest…
and let all the creation say, "Amen" and "Amen"!

Winder First Christian
May 18, 2014

Pastoral Prayer

God of grace, and God of glory
On thy people pour thy power

In weakness do we pray for strength. In solitude do we pray for community. In darkness do we pray for light. Come, Lord Jesus, and enliven us with your presence.

Some of us are so needy!
Some of us are so frightened!
Some of us are so lost!

Come, Lord Jesus, come!

Part the clouds, and let the day star show forth thy praise.
Let all that is praise thy name.

Tell us of thy light, and then let your candle set the galaxies aflame.

Speak words of hope in our silence.
Speak words of challenge to our timidity.
Speak words of blessing to the sick.
Speak words of comfort to the depressed.
Speak words of courage to those afraid to die.
Speak words of courage to those afraid to live.

Forgive us when we need it.

Lead us when we wander.

For our prayers are made in the Savior's name.

Alcovy Mt. Baptist Church
November 19, 2013

Pastoral Prayer

All Holy and all righteous God, hear us as we pray.
Hear us as we count our blessings, and give thee our
thankful hearts!
Hear our prayers of joyful praise!
Hear our prayers for the sick.
Bless those who have been sick a long time.
Bless those who seek help in emergency rooms.
Bless those who are frightened because of undiag-
nosed illness.
Hear our prayers for all caregivers.
Hear our prayers for our leaders:
Leaders in church
Leaders in government
Leaders in our communities
Leaders in our world.

Lead us all to feel a passion for justice, for peace, for
    beauty and grace. Hear all our prayers, for they
    are made in the savior's name.
Amen.

Alcovy Mountain Baptist Church
November 10, 2013 Morning

Pastoral Prayer

O thou who didst pray for "oneness" in the congregation of the righteous, we come into thy house with that same prayer on our lips. O great forgiving God, give us enough love to make reconciliation a reality.

Take away our rest, Lord, until we all rest in thee.

Take away our peace, Lord, until we all find peace with thee.

Bless all those who need thy nearness.

Bless the medical professionals who often stop the pain and bring hope.

Trouble those in power who deem it no sin to take advantage of position.

Trouble those who are careless and callous in their dealings with the weak and the poor and the lost.

Hear all our prayers, for they are made in the Savior's name.

Amen.

October 20, 2013
Morning Prayer

All holy and righteous God, we enter thy house this day with praise and thanksgiving. Thy blessings flow through our days, and our gratitude is real, yet unequal to thy love. So let this worship hour be for each of us a joy and a blessing and a challenge.

Giver of light and life and, Lord, even of the darkness, we do beseech thee to hear our prayers.

Forgive our sins.

Heal the sick.

Comfort the dying.

Give solace to the bereaved.

Give shalom to the fearful.

Let your peace that passes all understanding reign supreme in our hearts.

For we make our prayer in the name of Him who taught us when we pray to say:

Our Father, who art in heaven, hallowed be thy name.

Thy kingdom come, thy will be done, on earth as it is in heaven.

Give us this day our daily bread.

And forgive us our trespasses,

as we forgive those who trespass against us.

And lead us not into temptation but deliver us from evil.

For thine is the kingdom and the power and the glory forever—

Amen.

A Time of Prayer in the Name
of Andrew Clifford Bell

As we are able, let us pray:

"God of grace and God of glory, on thy people pour thy power," find so the hymn goes. Powerful words, but not enough. We need so much more.

We need power—yes, and strength and hope and comfort and reassurance. And, most of all, for us and especially for Andrew, grant a double portion of thy peace.

In a world like ours, nothing is more scarce than peace. All of us long for it. Few there be who ever find it.

So tune us, Dear Lord, that we might hear the truths which can give us comfort, truths which can give us peace.

Listen now, it is God's message to each one of us:

"O love that wilt not let me go,

I rest my weary soul in thee…"

Perhaps we can make better sense of it all if we can grasp the truth that Andrew has chosen to "rest his weary soul" in eternity.

God bless him on his journey.

God bless us with the peace that can send him on his way.

In the name of the God of peace, hear our prayers.

Amen.

A Service in the Name of James Tyree Manley

It is finished! The old promises have been read and proclaimed. Prayers have been offered, born to lift us up into the very presence of the Almighty.

One question remains, quietly gnawing away at the tenderloin of our souls—is it true? Are the promises of God true? Do we recount the stories and the preaching and the ceremony to calm our own fears? Are the promises really true?

Proof falls away on either side. There is no proof! But we folk of the faith are not abandoned into darkness. There is a reality beyond mathematics. It is a reality called faith and grace and love. In them lies our hope—our hope about life and death and immortality.

We do here and now claim that hope, and these promises, in the strong name of James Tyree Manley, born to be a pastor and a counselor, a husband and father. He remained true to his calling 'til the day he died.

We are made stronger by his faith, and we hold tightly to its truths. Hear the Gospel of John's words of life:

> For God so loved the world that He gave His only Son, that whoever believes in Him should not perish, but have everlasting life.
>
> For God sent not His Son into the world to condemn the world, but that the world through Him might be saved. (John 3:13–17)

Jesus as Savior and Lord! If these words of John are not true, then there is no spiritual reality. All is futile and lost and empty, and darkness will rule forever and forever more.

Jesus as Savior and Lord! If these words are true, let the shouting begin. If these words are true, rejoice! We are a part of His kingdom! We have been called from the four corners of creation to swell the mighty chorus.

Hosanna, Hosanna, holy is His name! Sacred is His theme.

Praise Him!

Praise Him 'til time becomes eternity, and all shadows are banished.

Praise Him!

> Immortal, invisible, God only wise.
>
> In light inaccessible-hid from our eyes.
>
> Most blessed, most glorious, the Ancient of Days. Almighty, victorious. Thy great name we praise!
>
> (W.C. Smith, 1867)

And all of the faithful gathered said, "Amen!"

(Friends and Family,

This brief meditation was given at the service of internment for James's ashes. The service was held on the grounds of MacAfee School of Theology on November 14, 2014.

The words for this meditation did not come easily for me, and in getting the final copy ready for saving, I have made some additions and changes. The most obvious being the addition of the first verse of "Immortal, Invisible." I believe its glorious word pictures have a place here, and James would certainly not mind. I hope everyone else who chances to read this will be as understanding.

James's Brother, Clay)

Funeral Service

And so we are gathered to praise God in the name of, to the memory of _____. It is a service of reflection. It is a service of tears. It is a service of laughter. Laughter? How can that be unless we simply deny the obvious? No matter what we do, we are in the presence of the reality of death. Is laughter really appropriate here and now?

Only if we have heard the promises and claimed them.

Only if we have heard the Master's voice and believed Him.

Only if we have felt the Master's presence and known him for who he is—even the Prince of Peace, the Son of God, the Savior of the world, our risen, reigning Lord.

The promises we have heard since childhood. Our sins, though real, are forgiven for the asking. There is saving power in the name of Jesus of Nazareth. Life everlasting is freely available to all. The Holy Spirit is the comforting presence which warms our hearts even when life deals us the most cruel, the most undeserved of harsh blows. At the sound of the trumpet, resurrection morning will shout open the doors of heaven, and the grave will hold none of the children of God.

So many promises—do you believe that they are true? Can we depend on God in the presence of death? There is no objective proof of the validity of the divine promises, the divine presence. We have access to the promises only through belief and faith. The old hymn says:

Only believe, only believe all things are possible
Only believe.
It is worthy of our thanksgiving and praise.
For by grace are you saved through faith,
and that not of yourselves, it is the gift of God.

Believe in His name! Have faith! His grace is his love, and it is free to all!

So come to the mercy seat! Come and confess! Come and believe! Come and accept! Come and trust! And then and only then can we worship in the presence of death and laugh. Oh, I know that tears are appropriate. Only the coldest of hearts will not acknowledge our loss. But the loss of death is not the whole story, and it is not the end of the story. Hear the promises, and through faith claim them for your own.

Then we can sit around the kitchen table and tell stories about _____ stories about her/his love of family and flowers, stories about her/his quick wit and gales of laughter. So many memories. It is not easy to laugh and cry at the same time, but you can.

Amen.

God's Word for a Fear-Filled World

Peace I leave with you, my peace I give to you.

(John 14:27)

Let not your hearts be troubled, neither let them be afraid.

(John 14:1)

Since we are justified by faith, we have peace with God.

(Romans 5:1)

Grace to you and peace from God our Father.

(Colossians 1:2)

Let the peace of Christ rule in your hearts."

(Colossians 3:15)

For He (Christ Jesus) is our peace, who has made us all one.

(Ephesians 2:14)

And now may the God of peace, who brought again from the dead our Lord Jesus, that great shepherd of the sheep, through the blood of the everlasting covenant, make you perfect to do his will, working in you that which is pleasing in his sight, through Jesus Christ to whom be glory forever and ever. Amen! (Hebrews 13:20–21)

Credits

Photographs of churches

Oakhurst Baptist Church, photo and permission to use made by Gail L. Bell.

Loganville Christian Church, photo by Gloria Bienstock.

Permission by Gloria and the pastor.

Northside Drive Baptist Church, photo and permission to use it given by Andrew H. Gee. Permission also from Rev. Dr. James Lamkin to use photo of the church sanctuary.

North Clarendon Baptist Church, photo taken from church brochure, sent to us by the church secretary with permission to use.

Biographical Sketch

W m. Clay Manley
3535 Youth-Monroe Road
Loganville, GA 30052–4328

Born 12/17/1935 in Milan, Tennessee
Most of my life has been spent in the Atlanta, GA
area.

Education:
Campbell High School, Smyrna, GA
Georgia Tech (1952–1954)
BA in English Literature, Mercer University
(1954–1957)
MDiv from Union Theological Seminary, New
York City (1959–1962)

Experience:
Two years student pastor while attending Mercer
Two years pastor, Briarlake Baptist Chapel
Five years pastor, Woodstock Baptist Church

Two years interim pastor, Oakhurst Baptist Church
Three years pastor, Trinity Baptist Church,
    Conyers, GA
One year interim pastor, High Point Baptist Church,
    Covington, GA
Five years pastor, Loganville Christian Church
    (Disciples of Christ), Loganville, GA

Non Church-related work experience:
Real estate brokerage

Personal:
Married to Theresai Mann Manley in 1957. She is a
    1956 BA graduate of Mercer University.
Three children, five grandchildren, and two
    great-granddaughters

About the Author

I am a retired Baptist minister. My heritage is Southern Baptist. My roots were nourished in the fields of evangelism, church growth, and denominational exclusivity. My "call" to preach was practically preordained.

The first defining moment in my religious pilgrimage was my enrollment at Mercer University, Macon, GA. The Christianity faculty was filled with bright, dedicated, inspiring teachers. They encouraged me to consider attending one of the seminaries in the Northeast. I chose Union Theological Seminary in New York City. I was looking for intellectual integrity and warm openness. I found both. Union Theological Seminary was at the very top of the intellectual ladder and the spiritual one, as well.

At the same time, I was warned by several Baptist ministers that my attending a non-Southern Baptist Seminary would preclude my pastoring a Southern Baptist Church. I did not believe, and did not heed, their advice. I could not make myself believe that the church I had grown up in had moved so far to the radical conservative "right" that I would no longer be welcome.

I was wrong. I soon learned that the Baptist Church of my youth no longer existed. Looking back, I can see several "roads not taken" which could have made a difference in my ministerial career. I just kept trying to be a Baptist Pastor, and that was the one thing the "powers that be" would not let me do.

The years go by at an ever increasing speed. And we can only do our best as opportunities present themselves.

Clay Manley